101 Inclusive
& SEN Science
& Computing
Lessons

also in the 101 Inclusive and SEN Lessons *series*

101 Inclusive and SEN English Lessons
Fun Activities and Lesson Plans for Children Aged 3–11
ISBN 978 1 78592 365 4
eISBN 978 1 78450 708 4

101 Inclusive and SEN Maths Lessons
Fun Activities and Lesson Plans for Children Aged 3–11
ISBN 978 1 78592 101 8
eISBN 978 1 78450 364 2

of related interest

Specific Learning Difficulties – What Teachers Need to Know
Diana Hudson
Illustrated by Jon English
ISBN 978 1 84905 590 1
eISBN 978 1 78450 046 7

Flying Starts for Unique Children
Top Tips for Supporting Children with SEN or Autism When They Start School
Adele Devine
ISBN 978 1 78592 001 1
eISBN 978 1 78450 241 6

Helping Children to Improve Their Gross Motor Skills
The Stepping Stones Curriculum
Rachel White
ISBN 978 1 78592 279 4
eISBN 978 1 78450 587 5

Creating Autism Champions
Autism Awareness Training for Key Stage 1 and 2
Joy Beaney
Illustrated by Haitham Al-Ghani
ISBN 978 1 78592 169 8
eISBN 978 1 78450 441 0

Roxy the Raccoon
A Story to Help Children Learn about Disability and Inclusion
Alice Reeves
Illustrated by Phoebe Kirk
ISBN 978 1 78592 451 4
eISBN 978 1 78450 828 9
Part of the *Truth & Tails* series

Okay Kevin
A Story to Help Children Discover How Everyone Learns Differently
James Dillon
Illustrated by Kara McHale
ISBN 978 1 78592 732 4
eISBN 978 1 78450 432 8

101 Inclusive
& SEN Science
& Computing
Lessons

FUN ACTIVITIES
& LESSON PLANS
for Children Aged 3–11

Claire Brewer and Kate Bradley

Jessica Kingsley *Publishers*
London and Philadelphia

First published in 2018
by Jessica Kingsley Publishers
73 Collier Street
London N1 9BE, UK
and
400 Market Street, Suite 400
Philadelphia, PA 19106, USA

www.jkp.com

Library of Congress Cataloging in Publication Data
A CIP catalog record for this book is available from the Library of Congress

British Library Cataloguing in Publication Data
A CIP catalogue record for this book is available from the British Library

ISBN 978 1 78592 366 1
eISBN 978 1 78450 709 1

Printed and bound in Great Britain

Contents

SECURING

COMPUTING

EMERGING

SECURING

Introduction

Hello and welcome to the third book in our '101 Inclusive and SEN Lessons' series!

While changes to school funding are affecting the way schools are able to support complex learners in classrooms, we remain passionate about ensuring children with special educational needs receive a broad, balanced, creative and accessible curriculum. With this book full of practical and exciting lessons we hope to support teachers, teaching assistants, parents and other professionals to include all children in their planning and teaching across an increasing range of curriculum subjects.

With the government accepting the recommendations of the Rochford Review, and P Levels no longer being a statutory assessment for children working below National Curriculum levels from September 2018,[1] we understand that many schools and practitioners may find that there are currently few options to replace them. Thus we feel that P Levels still offer an invaluable approach to structuring lessons and progression for children with SEN. The lessons in this book are still designed to meet the objectives set out in the P Level document.[2] However, these are simply a guideline to direct adults working with complex learners to choose lessons that are appropriate to the child's current level of understanding and development. Consequently the lessons in this book are divided into subsections to help guide you to select the most appropriate objectives for the learners you are working with: 'Emerging' relates to P Levels 4 and 5, 'Developing' relates to P Levels 5 and 6, and 'Securing' relates to P Level 8.

Each chapter starts with lesson objectives designed for the most complex learners and then works up towards more challenging objectives. Plenaries have

---

1   Standards and Testing Agency (2016) *Rochford Review: Final Report.* London: DfE.
2   Department for Education & Standards and Testing Agency (2017) *Performance (P Scale) Attainment Targets For Pupils With Special Educational Needs.* London: DfE.

been included for each lesson in order to provide an obvious end point for the child. We have included ideas for ways to consolidate learning. As for children with SEN, doing an activity once is unlikely to support their understanding of a concept.

The book also includes a chapter of starters designed to engage children in motivating learning styles from the beginning of each lesson. It is up to you to decide which starters suit which lesson you are teaching, as you may want to meet a range of additional skills in one session.

We love teaching science to all the learners we work with as there are so many ways to explore the world we live in through scientific experiments at all stages of learning. Working using a 'scientific method', i.e. hypothesising, experimenting and evaluating, supports children to develop problem-solving and generalisation skills. In this book we have drawn on our extensive teaching experience to create exciting, sometimes explosive, science lessons that aim to develop children's love of exploring their environment through working in a more organised, 'scientific' way.

Computing offers the learners we work with many ways to access their environment and widen their range of experiences. Through appropriate use of the Internet and devices such as tablets, children with additional needs can often develop new ways of learning and communicating. In this book we have tried to ensure that the lessons in the Computing chapter encompass a broad range of information and communication technology (ICT) equipment such as cameras, tablets, remote control cars, walkie-talkies and communication switches. Many of the lessons are designed to develop key skills that support children to develop communication and independent learning strategies such as understanding cause and effect and using ICT to interact with classmates and adults.

We have both used many of these ideas in our classrooms and wider practice and hope that you enjoy teaching with them in yours!

Claire and Kate

Follow and share your ideas with us: @clairebrewers, @Kate_Brads

What Do We Mean By Additional Skills?

- Kinaesthetic: movement is important to stimulate the child and provide learning experiences that do not revolve around sitting at a table and chair.

- Auditory: being able to develop listening and processing skills in a variety of subjects across the school day will support children to become more attentive in lessons and life.

- Fine motor: these are the skills that involve doing activities on a smaller scale. Developing these skills supports handwriting, dressing and manipulation in the long term.

- Gross motor: these involve the big muscle groups in the body and are large-scale movements. Developing these skills supports trunk control, coordination and motor planning.

- Tactile: skin covers the entirety of the body and is the largest sensory system. Having difficulties processing tactile input (such as getting messy) means that the children don't explore and experience the world to its full potential.

- Attention: a child's ability to attain and engage in activities to their full extent needs time and patience. The ability to focus on an individual activity for a longer period of time enables learning to take place. By providing exciting, short activities you can build a child's tolerance to this.

- Communication: with reference to communication, this is about receptive (listening to) and expressive (responding to) language. Language does not have to be speech – it can be in the form of visuals, switches and gesture.

- Social communication: this is about the vital skills of sharing time and experience with a partner, turn taking and knowing rules within social situations and games.

Resources

This is not an exhaustive list, but where possible we have used resources that we find easily in our own classrooms so that life is not made harder for you by having to go out of your way to prepare extra resources for the lessons. Please note that some items such as vinegar and bicarbonate of soda are safe to touch but not to ingest, so close adult supervision will be required when using some of the resources throughout this book.

Resources that you will use throughout the book:

- communication switches such as Big Mack switches (referred to in the book as 'switches')

- access to printers, photocopiers, interactive whiteboards (IWBs)

- headphones

- electronic tablets

- Internet access

- builder's trays

- choosing board (large firm board with strips of Velcro to attach symbols and pictures)

- laminating sheets and access to a laminator

- water and sand trays

- messy media e.g. flour, cornflour, shaving foam, play foam

- small world characters including animals and mini-beasts

- cars

- trains

- whiteboard and pens

- chalk

- felt-tip pens

- pencils

- tape – clear, masking, etc.

- sensory toys (flashing balls, massage cream, hand massagers)

- canvas bags

- tidy up box

- scissors

- boxes

- magnets

- bicarbonate of soda

- vinegar

- clear plastic bottles

- water-spray bottles

- aprons

- food colouring

- musical instruments

- remote control cars

- walkie-talkies

- a range of wind-up toys

- planting materials – soil, seeds, pots, etc.

- baking materials – ingredients, bowls, spoons, etc.

- pipettes

- torches

- coloured acetate

- balloons

- building blocks.

STARTERS

Stop Go Switches

RESOURCES

One switch with the word 'stop' pre-recorded and a 'stop' symbol on top

One switch with the word 'go' pre-recorded and a 'go' symbol on top

Large pocket dice with action symbols e.g. jump, hop, clap, spin, start jump, wave

ACTIVITY

- Support the children to sit in a semicircle.

- Adult models rolling the dice, doing the action shown and then pressing the 'stop' and 'go' switches to control their actions.

- Give the 'stop' switch to one child and the 'go' switch to another child.

- Choose another child to come to the front, roll the dice and identify the action.

- Support the children to control the action of the child in the middle by using the 'stop' and 'go' switches.

- Swap around so everyone has a turn rolling the dice and operating the switches.

Teaching note: this activity could also be done with music rather than actions.

Bean Bag Topple

RESOURCES

One beanbag per child

Several building blocks (ideally fairly large, soft play cubes)

ACTIVITY

- The children sit in a small group in a semicircle.

- At the front, adult builds a tall tower with the building blocks.

- The children each have a turn throwing the beanbag at the tower to see if they can knock it down to observe the effect of their actions.

Fast or Slow Dice

RESOURCES

One large pocket dice with action symbols

One large pocket dice with fast and slow symbols

ACTIVITY

- Once the children are sat in a semicircle ask two children to come to the front.

- Support Child A to roll the action symbol dice, identify the action and then to do the action.

- Child B rolls the fast and slow dice, and directs their friend to do the action either fast or slow according to how the dice lands.

- Repeat until all the children have had a turn completing the action and directing their friends.

Tactile Feely Bag

RESOURCES

One non-transparent bag (feely bag)

A range of rough and smooth objects e.g. pine cones, sticks, pebbles

Laminated rough and smooth symbols placed on a choosing board

ACTIVITY

- Once the children are sat in a semicircle sing the feely bag song to the tune of 'Jingle Bells': 'Feely bag, feely bag, what's inside the feely bag? Put your hand in, feel about, when you're ready pull something out!'

- Present the feely bag to one of the children and support them to pull an object out and explore.

- Support the child to indicate whether it is rough or smooth by matching it to the correct symbol.

- Repeat until all the children have had a turn.

Teaching note: the items in the feely bag can be adapted according to the lesson or topic e.g. big/small, wet/dry, float/sink, magnetic/non-magnetic, fruit/not fruit.

What Will Happen?

RESOURCES

One clear balloon

Funnel

Glitter

ACTIVITY

- Support the children to sit in a semicircle.

- Adult shows the children the balloon, explains they are going to blow it up and asks 'What will happen?' Support the children to guess what will happen e.g. will it get bigger, pop, change colour?

- Adult shows the children the funnel, places the balloon around the end of the funnel and then pours in the glitter. Adult asks again 'What will happen?' and supports children to comment.

- Adult blows up the balloon and stops after a couple of breaths and asks 'What has happened?' Again support children to respond e.g. the balloon is bigger, can see inside.

- Once the balloon is blown up, adult explains they are going to let go! Again ask the children 'What will happen?' and support to comment e.g. it will get smaller, the glitter will go everywhere, be messy.

- Let go of the balloon and watch what happens. Adult picks up the deflated balloon and asks again 'What happened?'

Teaching note: as this starter is repeated children will be able to respond to the question with decreased prompting. Other media can also be poured into the balloon such as flour or even water!

In the Hoop

RESOURCES

Large hoops

Posters of 'hard', 'soft' and 'wet'

Bag of hard, soft or wet items or pictures depicting them

ACTIVITY

- Place all of the items in the bag and lay the hoops out in a large space on the floor, place a poster in each of the hoops to label it.

- Pull an item from the bag and ask the children to run to the hoop that best describes the item.

- Repeat.

- Ask a child to come and choose an item from the bag; everyone runs to the hoop and the child takes the item with them and places it in the hoop.

- Repeat until all items are used.

- At the end of the game, talk to the children about how they have 'sorted' the items. What do they notice?

Odd One Out

RESOURCES

Three pictures

ACTIVITY

- Sit as a group and show the children the three pictures.

- Ask them to tell you which one is the odd one out and why.

- Take turns with offering suggestions.

- Ensure the children know that there is no wrong or right answer.

Teaching note: start simply with three pictures where there is a connection of some kind, such as the colour or type. A suggestion may be a red car, a red bike and a red apple. As the children get used to this speaking and listening activity, the pictures can be made slightly more challenging.

Bubbletastic

RESOURCES

Two washing up bowls

Water

Washing up liquid

Glycerine

Bubble wands

Visual instructions for making bubble mix

ACTIVITY

- Prepare a bubble mixture with 125ml of washing up liquid, 1.25l water and two tablespoons of glycerine. Do not over-mix.

- Place this in front of the group, give each member a bubble wand and allow a few minutes' exploration. Tell the children they are going to make their own mix.

- Provide the visual instructions, materials and washing up bowl for the children to make a mixture of their own.

- Give them the wands back and allow them to try their own mix.

- Place both washing up bowls out so that lots of bubbles can be blown!

Spaghetti Bridge

RESOURCES

Dry spaghetti

Building blocks

Pictures of bridges

ACTIVITY

- Give each child a piece of dry spaghetti and ask them to break it. This should happen easily.

- Show the children a picture of a bridge, and tell them that you want them to use spaghetti to build the bridge.

- Adult to place two blocks face down on the floor so the spaghetti can rest on top. Start laying spaghetti on.

- Give each child spaghetti and blocks and ask them to make one too.

- Once lots of spaghetti has been placed down, start adding the bricks on top to build a structure or tower. If there is enough spaghetti, it should hold!

Space Bottles

RESOURCES

Empty plastic water bottles with lids

Jugs

Glitter

Pipettes

Sequins

Oil

Food colouring

Sellotape

ACTIVITY

- Prior to the session, make a space bottle by adding water and glitter to a bottle. Tape the lid so that it is secure.

- Show this to the children, and tell them they can make one.

- Place the resources out on the table and give each child an empty bottle. Allow them to explore putting in different amounts of resources.

- Once everyone has finished, turn off the lights, put some calm music on and spend time exploring the bottles.

SCIENCE

1. Push Me Pull Me Planting

Learning Objective

Emerging

Pupils cause movement by a pushing or pulling motion.

Additional Skills

Gross motor: grasping and pulling plants.

Fine motor: using pincer grip to pick up seeds.

Tactile: exploring different textures such as soil.

Resources

Soil in a container (or planting area)

Seeds

Pre-planted flowers/ grass/weeds

MAIN

- Adult supports the child to explore the different seeds and then models using a pincer grip to pick up a seed and push it in the soil.

- Adult then supports child to use pincer grip to pick up a seed and push it in the soil, all the while singing, to the tune of the 'Hokey Cokey', 'Pick the seed up in your fingers and push it in the soil (x3), that's what it's all about!'

- Next, adult encourages child to explore the pre-planted flowers/grass/weeds and then models pulling them out of the soil.

- Adult supports child to pull the flowers/grass/weeds out of the soil, all the while singing, to the tune of the 'Hokey Cokey', 'Find the flowers/grass/weeds in the soil and pull them all up (x3), that's what it's all about!'

PLENARY

Encourage the child to stand with others in a circle and sing 'Ring a Ring o' Roses' together and model 'pushing' back into a standing position after 'we all fall down'!

CONSOLIDATION ACTIVITIES

Use the terms 'push' and 'pull' in other contexts across the child's day e.g. when playing with cars model 'pushing' them forwards and 'pulling' them back.

2. Tug of War

Learning Objective

Emerging

Pupils cause movement by a pushing or pulling motion.

Additional Skills

Gross motor: gripping and pulling different materials.

Tactile: exploring different textured materials.

Social communication: taking part in a game with another person.

Resources

Range of different materials that can be pulled e.g. scarf, rope, paper, play dough

MAIN

- Adult supports the child to explore the different materials and then models pulling the materials to see what happens.

- Adult holds one end of a material and supports the child to hold the other end of the material and encourages them to 'pull' (a second adult may need to support this until the child becomes familiar with the lesson).

- Try this with a range of materials and encourage the child to notice differences between the materials.

PLENARY

Adult shows the child all the materials again and supports them to make a choice for their preferred material that can be explored again.

CONSOLIDATION ACTIVITIES

Try this activity in other areas such as the sensory room (if one is available) so that the tug of war can be more dramatic e.g. letting go and letting child fall back onto the soft matting, or child can 'pull' themselves up onto different areas of the room.

3. Tall Towers

Learning Objective

Emerging

Pupils explore objects and materials provided, changing some materials by physical means and observing the outcomes.

Additional Skills

Fine motor: using pincer grip to join blocks together.

Attention: maintaining attention on an adult-directed activity for 5 minutes.

Gross motor: large swiping motions for knocking down towers.

Resources

Large building blocks (ideally blocks with smooth sides or soft play cubes)

Finished box

MAIN

- Adult supports the child to explore the blocks and then models building a tall tower.

- Adult counts down '5, 4, 3, 2, 1, uh ohhhhhh!' to build anticipation and then knocks down the tower, modelling language that highlights the outcomes of actions.

- Adult encourages the child to build a tall tower, wait for the countdown and then knock down the tower.

- Repeat this activity, each time noticing the change from the bricks being together in the tower to being separate when knocked down.

PLENARY

At the end of the lesson adult counts down '5, 4, 3, 2, 1, tall towers has finished, time to tidy up.' Adult supports the child to place bricks back in the box, noticing each time where the block is placed in the box.

CONSOLIDATION ACTIVITIES

Repeat this activity in other spaces with different sized and textured cubes e.g. large, soft, play-style cubes in the playground or soft playroom.

4. Body Part Rap

Learning Objective

Emerging

Pupils make sounds using their own bodies and imitate or copy sounds.

Additional Skills

Auditory: recognising familiar sounds.

Social communication: working with a partner.

Attention: maintaining attention to complete an activity for 5 minutes.

Resources

Three recording devices such as switches

Tablet or other video recording device

Laminated photos of hands, feet and mouth

MAIN

- Adult sits opposite the child and explains, 'We are going to make sounds with our bodies.'

- Adult makes sounds with their mouth and encourages child to imitate the sound or create their own sound. Record this on one of the devices.

- Next, adult makes sounds with their hands e.g. clapping and banging on table, and again encourages child to imitate or make their own sound. Record this on another device.

- Next, adult makes sounds with their feet e.g. stamping, and again encourages the child to imitate or make their own sound. Record this sound on the final device.

- Support the child to play back the sounds they made with their body by e.g. pressing the switch down.

- Each time the child plays a sound, show them the corresponding photo.

- Encourage the child to play back the sounds in different orders and either child or adult names each body part as the sound is played to make a body part rap.

- Video record the rap!

PLENARY

Watch the video back with the child and encourage them to use their different body parts to copy the sounds again.

CONSOLIDATION ACTIVITIES

Across the day encourage the child to imitate or copy sounds that the adult makes; e.g. to join in when clapping a classmate's achievement, to cheer as part of a crowd at an appropriate time.

5. Copy My Move!

Learning Objective

Emerging

Pupils imitate actions involving Main body parts.

Additional Skills

Social communication: playing as part of a small group.

Visual: watching another's action and then imitating that action.

Kinaesthetic: moving different body parts.

Resources

Enough space to stand in a small circle

MAIN

- In a small group, adult supports the children to stand in a circle. Adult asks one child to stand in the middle of the circle and, using the child's name, sings, to the tune of 'Brown Girl in the Ring': 'Evie's in the ring tra la la la la, there's Evie in the ring tra la la la la, Evie in the ring tra la la la la, she looks like a sugar in a plum, plum plum! Show me your motion tra la la la la, Come on show me your motion tra la la la la, show me your motion tra la la la la she looks like a sugar in a plum, plum plum!'

- Encourage the child in the middle to make a movement e.g. jumping, stamping feet, clapping, and support the children around the edge to imitate the movement.

- Ask the child who was in the middle to choose the next person to go in the middle of the ring and repeat the activity again.

PLENARY

To finish the activity encourage the children to stand in a line and copy adult's movements to 'cool down' e.g. taking a deep breath and touching toes, stretching arms in front.

CONSOLIDATION ACTIVITIES

Build into the daily routine times to imitate actions; e.g. just before lunch find a video on the interactive whiteboard of a song such as 'Head, Shoulders, Knees and Toes' and support the child to imitate the actions.

6. Dark Fortress

Learning Objective

Emerging

Pupils communicate their awareness of changes in light, sound or movement.

Additional Skills

Communication: using vocalisation or speech, communicate awareness of changes in light.

Social communication: working alongside another person.

Tactile: exploring changes to environment.

Resources

Table

Large pieces of material/ blankets

Torches

Coloured acetate

MAIN

- Set up the activity by placing the large pieces of material or blankets over the table to make a dark fort and place the sheets of coloured acetate in the fort.

- Adult explains to the child that we are going to explore light and dark, and models how to use the torch. Support the child to turn the torch on and off.

- Adult encourages the child to turn the torch on and explore the dark fortress, and use language such as 'light' and 'dark' to label the changes.

- Once in the fort explore turning the torch on and off, noticing the child's reaction to the changes.

- Explore placing the torch behind the coloured acetate and changing the colour of the light in the fort.

- Support the child to explore and notice the changes in the light.

PLENARY

With the child, turn the torches on and off in the dark fortress and sing 'Twinkle, Twinkle, Little Star' and then count down '5, 4, 3, 2, 1, dark fort has finished, let's turn on the lights!' Come out from the fort and return the torches to their box.

CONSOLIDATION ACTIVITIES

When entering other rooms in the building, support the child to notice if they are dark or light; support child to turn lights on if needed and notice the change in the room.

7. What Can I Find?

Learning Objective

Emerging

Pupils explore objects and materials provided.

Additional Skills

Visual: searching for appropriate content.

Social communication: working alongside others.

Fine motor skills: manipulating objects.

Resources

Builder's tray

Range of materials (fabrics, pine cones, wooden spoons, metal spoons, glitter, etc.)

Basket or container for each child

MAIN

- Place a builder's tray on a table in the centre of the room.
- Place onto it lots of different materials.
- Place a large cover over the table.
- Give each child in the group a basket.
- Draw the children over to the table by showing excitement about what is underneath; adult to sneak a look.
- The adult then counts down and says 'wow' once the cover is removed.
- Children to be allowed time to explore the materials and fill their baskets; transport the materials to other parts of the room.
- The adult's role is key: you work alongside the children and follow their lead. Very minimal language is used. Try not to lead or direct the child's exploration; allow them to investigate as independently as possible.

PLENARY

Count down '5, 4, 3, 2, 1' and sing a tidy-up song. Encourage the children to collect resources that they may have transported around the classroom.

CONSOLIDATION ACTIVITIES

Carry out this activity a few times within a week or across a few sessions in a term so that the children get used to being able to explore the materials. Each time, keep the materials the same, but add something new. See if the children gravitate to the same items, or if they are drawn in by the new things added.

8. Shake It Up

Learning Objective

Emerging

Pupils explore objects and observe outcomes.

Additional Skills

Visual: observing the changes.

Social communication: working alongside others.

Fine motor: spooning flour into the bags.

Tactile: touching new textures.

Resources

Builder's tray

Bowl, spoon and jug for each group member

Aprons

Zip-lock bags

Cornflour

Food colouring

MAIN

- Place a builder's tray on a table in the centre of the room.

- Give everyone in the group an apron. Roll up sleeves or if possible take off tops with long sleeves.

- Give each child in the group a bowl of cornflour and a spoon.

- Allow them some time to explore this.

- After a few minutes give each child a zip-lock bag.

- Adults to model spooning the cornflour into the bag.

- Allow children time to try this themselves. If the cornflour has been spilt, the adults can go around and add some to each of the bags.

- Move all the bowls and spoons out of the tray.

- Lead adult to place a large jug in front of them. Show the children the different colours that can be added. Ask someone to choose a colour. Add the food colouring to the water.

- Adult to model pouring some of the water into the zip-lock bag. Seal the bag and then say 'shake, shake, shake'.

- Each child to be given a small container of water and they are encouraged to ask for the colour that they want. This needs to be added to the bags.

- The children can then either explore directly in the bag or get messy, or seal the bag and move the mixture around through the safety of the bag if they are tactile-defensive.

PLENARY

Count down '5, 4, 3, 2, 1' and sing a tidy-up song. Support everyone to wash his or her hands while an adult clears the equipment away.

8. Shake It Up *cont.*

CONSOLIDATION ACTIVITIES

Once they have been cleaned on the outside, stick the zip-lock bags with tape to a window. The children can then come and move the mixture around, and explore and observe the effects of mixing the cornflour with water.

9. Solid Shapes

Learning Objective

Emerging

Pupils explore objects and materials.

Additional Skills

Visual: observing the changes.

Social communication: working alongside others.

Tactile: touching new textures.

Resources

Light-box or a clear plastic box with lid, with fairy lights inside

Plastic box

Selection of solid objects (pencils, books, Duplo, etc.)

Selection of objects light will go through (coloured acetate, sweet wrappers, leaves, etc.)

MAIN

- Place the light-box in a prominent place in the room.
- Place the container of objects next to the light-box.
- Leave the children to explore the different materials.
- After the children have had time to explore, adult to place only solid objects on the light-box.
- Observe what the children do.
- The adult to place three transparent objects onto the light-box.
- Adult to offer the child a 'solid' and 'transparent' item that they can choose to place on the light-box.
- Allow the children to bring objects from around the room and to transport objects away to other places.

PLENARY

Count down '5, 4, 3, 2, 1' and sing a tidy-up song. All materials to go back into the box.

CONSOLIDATION ACTIVITIES

As the children's experience of science and exploration grows, the light-box can be used in other science lessons as an alternative means to explore objects, e.g. metals and natural items such as leaves and bark.

10. Lights Please

Learning Objective

Emerging

Pupils communicate their awareness of changes in light.

Additional Skills

Visual: observing the changes in light.

Attention: sharing an activity with an adult.

Fine motor: controlling the torch on and off.

Resources

Tent or fabric to create a den

Torches

Coloured A4 acetate sheets (red, yellow and blue)

Large pocket dice with red, yellow and blue inserts

MAIN

- Set up a tent in the room, or using materials cover tables so that there is a dark space.

- Place the box of torches and coloured acetate in the tent.

- Encourage the children to go into the tent and explore turning the torches on and off, and using the coloured acetate to change the colour of the light.

- Take the large dice into the tent.

- Roll the dice and name the colour that it lands on. Adult to choose the colour acetate and turn the torchlight the matching colour.

- Continue to roll the dice and change the colour of the light. Encourage the children to roll the dice or to select a colour acetate that the dice face can be matched to.

PLENARY

Count down '5, 4, 3, 2, 1' and sing a tidy-up song. All materials to go back into the box.

CONSOLIDATION ACTIVITIES

This can start off with just the primary colours for the first few times. Over time, add secondary colours to the dice and model to the children placing the red and yellow acetate onto each other so that the light turns orange.

11. Push Me Pull Me

Learning Objective

Emerging

Pupils cause movement by a pushing or pulling action.

Additional Skills

Visual: avoiding obstacles.

Attention: sharing an activity with an adult or peer.

Gross motor: pulling fabric.

Resources

Large box

Large fabrics and pieces of material

MAIN

- In the school hall ideally, or if not, in the classroom with all the furniture moved to the side, place the box of fabrics.

- Adult to place one of the fabrics on the floor, and support a child to lie on their tummy on the fabric.

- Adult pulls the fabric (and child) along, saying 'pull, pull'.

- Take turns swapping over the children and the fabric.

- Some of the fabric will glide much easier on the floor than others: the children will experience this.

- Encourage the children to pull the fabric with the adult and, eventually, by themselves.

- This activity requires close adult supervision at all times.

PLENARY

After everyone has had turns and carried out lots of pull motions, encourage the children to lie down on a piece of fabric and roll them up like a sausage roll and back again. Then count down '5, 4, 3, 2, 1' and finish the activity.

CONSOLIDATION ACTIVITIES

As children become familiar with the pull movement, other equipment can be added (such as the roll or perhaps a scooter board) so that there can be a push, allowing children to explore the movements by both carrying out the action or being involved in receiving the action.

12. Dig Deeper

Learning Objective

Emerging

Pupils take part in activities focused on the anticipation of environments.

Additional Skills

Visual: searching and locating objects.

Attention: sustaining attention for an extended period.

Gross motor: digging.

Communication: sharing with an adult what they have found.

Resources

Space to dig (or builder's tray and compost)

Aprons

Buckets

Spades

MAIN

- Ideally, find a space outdoors that can be used for digging. If this is not available, then set up a builder's tray with compost; you will need to add stones, twigs and bugs into this.

- Provide the children with an apron, suitable clothing if outdoors and a bucket and spade each.

- Adults in the group to work alongside the children and ensure that they stay safe (i.e. avoiding touching their mouths while dirty).

- Children to be given around 20 minutes to dig and explore. Adults to take interest in the objects that children find and share, but adults are not to try and lead any part of this discovery session.

PLENARY

After everyone has had a chance to explore, count the children down '5, 4, 3, 2, 1, finished' and take everyone to clean up and wash their hands.

CONSOLIDATION ACTIVITIES

If this session was outdoors, then using the items that the children found and placed in their buckets, a discovery table can be set up in the classroom. Include magnifying glasses, classification books and bug-catcher containers.

13. Search and Rescue

Learning Objective

Emerging

Pupils match objects in terms of single features.

Additional Skills

Visual: searching and locating objects.

Attention: sustaining attention for an extended period.

Tactile: distinguishing between different textures.

Communication: sharing with an adult what they have found.

Resources

Large cardboard box

Shredded paper

Soft toys (x6)

Hard toys (x6)

Visuals for 'hard' and 'soft'

MAIN

- Place all of the toys and shredded paper into the large box.

- Gather the child(ren) around the box and model searching through the paper and pulling out a toy; ensure that as the adult you act surprised!

- Name the toy (e.g. 'bear') and then touch it and say 'soft', placing it next to the 'soft' visual cue.

- Adult to sit back and say 'Your turn' to the child.

- Child to spend time searching through the box and finding the toys. Adult to model naming 'hard' and 'soft' if necessary.

PLENARY

After everyone has had a chance to explore, count the children down '5, 4, 3, 2, 1, finished' and ask the children to help put the paper and the toys back into the box.

CONSOLIDATION ACTIVITIES

To encourage the children to explore for themselves, set this activity up in a clear water tray so that the children can see the toys through the edges. Shredded paper is a safe texture; to add more of a challenge you could use flour or dry sand to hide the toys.

14. Let Me Out

Learning Objective

Emerging

Pupils indicate the before and after of material changes.

Additional Skills

Fine motor: using tools and spray bottles.

Attention: sustaining attention for the duration of a task.

Tactile: distinguishing between different textures.

Social communication: working with and alongside others.

Resources

Plastic containers of varying sizes

Small world toys (trains, cars, dinosaurs, LEGO® people, etc.)

Access to a freezer

Builder's tray

Toy toolkit

Water-spray bottles

MAIN

- The day before the lesson, place favourite toys into the plastic containers and fill them with water. You can also add food colouring and glitter to make them even more enticing. Place them in the freezer.

- Prior to the lesson, remove the plastic containers from the freezer and pop out the ice blocks onto a builder's tray. Place the toy tools and water-spray bottles with the ice on the tray. Finally write 'Help!' on a whiteboard and stand this in the middle of the tray.

- Allow the children time to see what has happened and to try a variety of ways to get the toys free from the ice.

- If the children want to collect other resources from around the class, this should be encouraged.

PLENARY

After everyone has had a chance to explore, count the children down '5, 4, 3, 2, 1, finished' and ask the children to put all the ice and toys in the sink ready to clean up.

CONSOLIDATION ACTIVITIES

If you are going to do this activity again, work with a few children on collecting toys that they want to be frozen. Let them try and fit them in different-sized boxes, etc. This will help them to understand the process of properties of materials.

15. Ready, Steady, Bake!

Learning Objective

Emerging

Pupils indicate the before and after of material changes.

Additional Skills

Fine motor: breaking eggs and mixing.

Visual: following simple instructions.

Attention: sustaining attention for the duration of a task.

Tactile: coping with mess on hands.

Social communication: working with and alongside others.

Resources

Simple fairy cake recipe from the Internet

Ingredients as per the recipe (i.e. flour, butter, eggs, sugar)

Bowls and spoons for each child

Aprons

Cake cases

Baking tray

Access to oven

MAIN

- Always check for allergies prior to any cooking sessions.

- Prior to the lesson, prepare a simplified version of the recipe and weigh out all the ingredients into individual bowls.

- Try and plan this lesson around a special occasion such as a birthday, or an event such as the school fair, so that the lesson also has purpose for the children.

- Let the children know that they are making fairy cakes today.

- Show them the recipe cards and the ingredients. Ask them all to wash their hands.

- Working either individually, or in twos, the children pour all the ingredients into the bowl in the correct order and mix.

- You can sing the mixing song 'Mix it round and round, mix it round and round, mix the mixture, mix the mixture, mix it round and round!' This helps ensure the children mix for longer than a few seconds.

- The adults may need to give the batter a mix before the children spoon the mixture into cake cases. Alert the children to the properties of the mixture, e.g. it is runny and wet.

- The children then place the cases onto a baking tray. If the oven is in the room, ask them if the oven will be hot or cold. When they say hot, you tell them that we have to be careful and that it is the adult's job.

- If the children are unlikely to wait for the duration of the baking, set a timer for 1 minute and produce the pre-baked cakes.

- If they can wait, then all clean up together while waiting.

15. Ready, Steady, Bake! *cont.*

PLENARY

After everyone has had a chance to explore, count the children down '5, 4, 3, 2, 1, finished', show the children the cakes and let them know they can decorate them when they are cold. Talk to the children about the cakes: are they still runny and wet?

CONSOLIDATION ACTIVITIES

Using icing sugar, water and food colouring, make different colour icing that the children can decorate their cakes with.

16. Something from Nothing

Learning Objective

Emerging

Pupils try out a range of equipment in familiar situations.

Additional Skills

Fine motor: scissor skills.

Visual: searching and locating materials.

Attention: sustaining attention for the duration of a task.

Social communication: working with and alongside others.

Resources

Newspaper, construction straws, straws, string, tape, masking tape, parcel tape, wool, cotton wool (and any items that you can find that the children can build with)

Scissors

Pictures of buildings

Visual instructions of simple projects to make

Table set up as 'creation table'

MAIN

- Place all the construction materials out on a table along with pictures and visual instructions of things the children can build, such as a picture of the Eiffel Tower or instructions on how to make a paper airplane.

- Invite the children to come and create.

- Adults to build alongside the children.

PLENARY

Once you have all been building for around 10 to 15 minutes, count the children down '5, 4, 3, 2, 1, finished'. Ask the children to place their models and work on the creation table and find their name label to go with their work.

CONSOLIDATION ACTIVITIES

This can be set up outside with lots of natural items such as stones, pens, twigs and twine. Encourage the children to bring their completed work to display on the creation table.

17. It Sticks

Learning Objective

Emerging

Pupils try out a range of equipment in familiar situations.

Additional Skills

Visual: searching and locating materials.

Attention: sustaining attention for the duration of a task.

Social communication: sharing resources with others.

Resources

Range of magnets

Builder's tray

Magnetic materials

Non-magnetic materials

Two boxes

Visuals of 'magnetic' and 'non-magnetic'

MAIN

- Place the magnetic and non-magnetic items on a tray with different sized and shaped magnets.
- Invite the children to explore the objects.
- After a few moments, adult to model using a magnet to find something magnetic. Show the children the visual of 'magnetic' and say, 'Look, magnetic.' Then adult to say to the children 'Your turn.'

PLENARY

Count the children down '5, 4, 3, 2, 1, finished'. Ask the children to place the magnetic items in the box. Then look at the items that are left on the table. Tell the children that these are non-magnetic. Place the non-magnetic items in a different box. Present two labels ('magnetic'/'non-magnetic') to one of the children and ask them to label the boxes.

CONSOLIDATION ACTIVITIES

Set up a magnetic construction kit for the children to explore and build with.

18. Where It Belongs

Learning Objective

Emerging

Pupils respond to simple scientific questions.

Additional Skills

Visual: searching and locating materials.

Tactile: touching and exploring a range of natural textures.

Social communication: sharing resources with others.

Communication: answering a question.

Resources

Range of natural materials (pine cones, soil, grass, leaves, flowers, twigs, etc.)

Builder's tray

Small world animals (fox, bird, hedgehog, mouse, badger, rabbit, etc.)

Visual question cards ('where?', 'find', 'show', etc.) plus visuals of each of the animals

MAIN

- Set up a natural-world builder's tray including all the resources that you have collected. Hide small word animals within the materials.

- Encourage the children to explore and manipulate the materials and animals.

- Adults to ask questions using the visuals such as 'Show me the flower', 'Find the bird' and 'Where is the hedgehog?'

PLENARY

Count the children down '5, 4, 3, 2, 1, finished'. Ask each child in turn to find and locate one of the animals and place this in the tidy up box.

CONSOLIDATION ACTIVITIES

Encourage the children to find natural materials while they are outside, which they can then place on the builder's tray to start making it their own creation.

19. Mini-Beast Match

Learning Objective

Emerging

Pupils match objects and materials in terms of single features or properties.

Additional Skills

Visual: recognising similarities.

Fine motor: using pincer grip to pick up plastic mini-beasts.

Attention: maintaining attention and completing an activity for 5 to 10 minutes

Resources

A selection of plastic mini-beasts

Two to four trays

Laminated symbols for colours of mini-beasts, 'wings' and 'no wings', numbers 0 to 6

MAIN

- To set up the activity, adult decides which single feature of the mini-beasts to focus on for this lesson ('wings' will be used as an example). In one tray place the laminated 'wings' symbol; in the other tray place the laminated 'no wings' symbol.

- Adult supports the child to choose a classmate to join them for the lesson.

- Adult supports the children to explore the plastic mini-beasts, commenting on whether or not the mini-beast has wings.

- Adult shows the children a mini-beast with wings and one without and explains to the children what wings are used for. Adult models placing the mini-beast with no wings in the tray with the corresponding symbol and then placing the one with wings in the tray with the 'wings' laminated symbol.

- Adult supports the children to work together to sort the remaining mini-beasts by the single feature of 'wings'.

PLENARY

Count how many mini-beasts have wings and how many don't have wings. Go outside and see if any mini-beasts with or without wings can be found.

CONSOLIDATION ACTIVITIES

Repeat this lesson over several sessions, choosing a different single feature each time e.g. sort by colour, number of legs.

20. Figure on the Floor

Learning Objective

Emerging

Pupils respond to simple scientific questions.

Additional Skills

Gross motor: awareness of whole body.

Social communication: working with a partner.

Communication: responding appropriately to a question.

Resources

Large pieces of paper (may need taping together to be large enough for child to lie on)

Marker pens

Two sets of symbols or words of body parts

MAIN

- Adult supports the child (Child A) to find a partner (Child B).

- Model the activity by asking Child B to lie down on the large piece of paper; adult takes a marker pen and draws around Child B, labelling body parts as they go e.g. 'Drawing around Alex's feet.'

- Support Child A to lie down on another large piece of paper and encourage Child B to draw around them, labelling body parts if possible.

- Next lay the two drawn figures next to each other and give the children the body part symbols/words.

- Ask the children 'Where is the head?' and encourage them to place the head symbol/word on the head of their drawn figure. Turn this into a race to see who can label the body part first!

PLENARY

If possible hang the figures on the wall so that other children can look at them too. Sit with the children and play another quick-fire game by saying 'Show meeee... hands!' and the children have to show the requested body part as quickly as possible.

CONSOLIDATION ACTIVITIES

Across other activities ask the child simple scientific questions such as, 'Is the towel wet or dry?' or 'What colour is the grass?'

21. Heartbeats

Learning Objective

Emerging

Pupils try out a range of equipment in familiar and relevant situations.

Additional Skills

Kinaesthetic: moving different body parts.

Social communication: working in a small group.

Tactile: experiencing changes in the sensory system.

Resources

Stethoscopes

Stopwatches

A4 laminated 'stop' and 'go' symbols

A4 laminated action symbols e.g. 'run', 'jump', 'climb', 'lie down'

A large space for exercising e.g. the hall

PE equipment such as A-frames, mats, trampoline

Parachute (optional)

MAIN

- In the hall children sit in a semicircle in a small group.

- Adult shows the children a stethoscope and models how it is used. Support the children to use the stethoscopes and listen to each other's heartbeats.

- Adult explains our heartbeat changes when we do exercise.

- Ask the children to stand up and then use an action symbol to instruct the children e.g. run. Use the stop and go symbols to support the instructions.

- After a short time running ask the children to come back and sit down. Use the stethoscopes again and see if the children notice a difference in their heart rate.

- Repeat this for other actions, each time stopping and using the stethoscope to listen to the change in heart rate.

- When the children are more familiar with this lesson support them to work with partners to use the stethoscopes, stopwatches and action symbols to instruct each other.

PLENARY

At the end of the session ask the children to lie down and relax. Play soothing music, maybe waft the parachute. Once the children have had several minutes to relax ask them to use the stethoscopes again to see how their heart rates have slowed down.

CONSOLIDATION ACTIVITIES

Repeat this activity in other areas using different exercise equipment such as in the playground or soft play room.

22. Dark Fortress 2

Learning Objective

Emerging

Pupils take part in activities focused on the anticipation of, and enquiry into, specific environments.

Additional Skills

Fine motor: operating equipment such as a torch.

Social communication: joining in with a game with another person.

Communication: commenting using gesture/vocalisation/ speech.

Resources

Table

Large pieces of material/ blankets

Torches

Toy versions of animals that live in/prefer the dark e.g. bear, owl, bat, certain mini-beasts

Laminated symbol bingo board of animals that will be in the dark fortress for each child

Dry wipe marker pen

MAIN

- Set up the activity by placing the large pieces of material or blankets over the table to make a dark fort and place the chosen toys in different areas in the fort (you may want to link these to your topic or a story such as 'Going on a Bear Hunt').

- Support the child to choose a classmate to join them for the lesson.

- Explain to the children that we are going on a hunt for animals that live in the dark! Show the children the symbol bingo board of the animals they will be looking for.

- Model for the children how to turn on the torch and use it to search for the animals.

- Go into the dark fortress together and use the torches to seek out the animals hiding in the dark.

- Encourage the children to comment when they find an animal.

PLENARY

Either in the dark fortress or back in the classroom, use a dry wipe marker pen to mark off the animals that were found in the dark.

CONSOLIDATION ACTIVITIES

Repeat this lesson for environments other than the 'dark', e.g. creatures that live in the sea (using the water tray and a net), and animals that live under straw.

23. Fruit and Veg Splat

Learning Objective

Emerging

Pupils indicate the 'before' and 'after' of material changes.

Additional Skills

Tactile: experiencing different fruit and vegetable textures.

Visual: recognising difference in colour before and after activity.

Gross motor: splat action.

Resources

Square pieces of white material

Range of fruit and vegetables that create colour e.g. beetroot, strawberries, blackberries

Laminated symbols to match fruit or vegetable

Laminated colour symbol corresponding to the colour produced by the fruit or vegetable

Laminated 'before' and 'after' symbols

MAIN

- Adult shows the children the different fruit and vegetables, matching them to their symbols. Encourage the children to feel and taste the fruit and vegetables.

- Adult models holding a piece of white material and naming it 'white'.

- Adult models placing the material on the floor and then placing e.g. a blackberry on top of the material.

- Adult holds their hand in the air and counts down '3, 2, 1, SPLAT!' and squashes the blackberry onto the material, releasing the juice and dying the material. Hold up the material and ask the children 'What colour is it now?' and support children to answer using speech or symbols.

- At the table support the children to explore changing the colour of the white material by 'splatting' different fruit and vegetables onto the material and indicating the change in colour using speech or symbols.

PLENARY

Adult holds up a piece of white material and asks 'Is this before or after fruit/veg splat?' and supports the children to use speech or symbols to answer. Hold up a fruit or vegetable-dyed piece of material and ask 'Is this before or after fruit/veg splat?' and again support to answer using speech or symbols. Repeat this for the different coloured pieces of material.

CONSOLIDATION ACTIVITIES

Encourage the child to notice colour changes at other times of the day e.g. before colouring on a piece of paper, and using chalk on the black playground floor.

24. Seasonal Signs

Learning Objective

Emerging

Pupils indicate the before and after of material changes.

Additional Skills

Kinaesthetic: going for a walk in the woods or local park.

Visual: noticing changes in the environment.

Attention: recalling events from previous experience.

Resources

Tablet or camera

Access to a local woodland or park (also appropriate risk assessment and permissions in line with school or setting policies)

Plastic bags for collecting leaves

Four large tree templates

Glue

MAIN

- In the autumn term plan to take the children in a small group on a walk to a local woodland or park to look at the leaves on the trees/ground. Before going on the walk prepare the children by explaining that we are going on a walk to look at the trees and find leaves to see how they look in autumn.

- While on the walk support the children to collect leaves and other autumnal plant life such as conkers. Encourage the children to comment on the properties of the leaves e.g. they are brown, crunchy.

- Support the child to use the camera to take photos of how the trees and leaves look in the autumn.

- When back at school, explore the leaves again and this time use the glue to stick them onto one of the four tree templates. Either adult or children write describing words around the tree e.g. 'brown', 'crunchy'.

- Print out the photos and place these around the tree template as well.

- Repeat this activity when it is winter, spring and summer and make a display of the tree templates on the wall.

PLENARY

After each woodland walk in the winter, spring and summer terms compare the new tree template with the one from the previous season. Encourage the child to notice the change in the leaves and how they were e.g. 'before winter and after spring'.

24. Seasonal Signs *cont.*

CONSOLIDATION ACTIVITIES

When exploring the outside environment encourage the child to notice the before and after of their surroundings: e.g. before the rain the grass was dry, and after it is wet; before the frost the playground was black, and after it is white; before the sun came out it was cold, and after it was hot.

25. It Swims It Runs

Learning Objective

Developing

Pupils recognise distinctive features of objects.

Additional Skills

Visual: searching and locating materials.

Tactile: touching and exploring a range of natural textures.

Social communication: sharing resources with others.

Communication: answering a question.

Resources

Two builder's trays

Small world animals for land (lion, elephant, dog, monkey, etc.)

Small world animals for sea (fish, dolphin, whale, jellyfish, etc.)

Large see-through box

Land and sea labels

Grass

Jug of water

Aprons

MAIN

- Place two large builder's trays on tables either side of a central table. On one builder's tray fill it with grass and label it 'land'. In the second builder's tray fill it with water and label it 'sea'. On the central table, place a large see-through box, and put all of the land and sea animals in the box.

- Give each child an apron so they can explore the grass and water, and ask them to sort the animals.

PLENARY

Count the children down '5, 4, 3, 2, 1, finished'. Ask each child in turn to find and locate one of the animals and place this in the tidy up box.

CONSOLIDATION ACTIVITIES

Carry out this activity a second time but in the see-through central box place animals, such as birds and crocodiles, that are not as obvious. Encourage the children to make a choice about where these animals might live. Then talk about it together.

26. Smooth and Silky

Learning Objective

Developing

Pupils recognise distinctive features of objects.

Additional Skills

Fine motor: using scissors and art materials.

Tactile: touching and exploring a range of natural textures.

Social communication: sharing resources with others.

Communication: using words to describe textures.

Resources

Pictures of snakes and hedgehogs

Two canvas bags

Art materials for a hedgehog

Art materials for a snake

Outlines of both animals

Glue

Scissors

Pens

Aprons

MAIN

- Prior to the lesson create two 'feely bags' – one containing art material for a hedgehog (hay, straws, art matchsticks, etc.) and one for a snake (silks, cotton wool, ribbons, etc.).

- Everyone to sit around a table; adult to show the children pictures of animals with contrasting textures, i.e. the hedgehog and the snake. Talk about what they might feel like.

- Pass around the feely bag for the hedgehog and use words such as 'spikey', 'hard' and 'rough'. Then repeat with the snake feely bag using words such as 'silky', 'soft' and 'smooth'.

- Provide each child with the choice of either a hedgehog or a snake outline, then allow the children time to create a spikey hedgehog or a smooth snake.

PLENARY

At the end of this, label each of the pieces of artwork with words the children say about their animal. Count the children down '5, 4, 3, 2, 1, finished'.

CONSOLIDATION ACTIVITIES

Carry out this activity a second time, adding more animals. Ask the children if they can find materials in the classroom that could be used in the feely bags.

27. Make It Sticky

Learning Objective

Developing

Pupils closely observe changes that occur.

Additional Skills

Fine motor: using spoons and spray bottles.

Tactile: touching and exploring a range of textures.

Social communication: sharing resources with others.

Communication: using key words to describe changes.

Resources

Plastic bowls

Wooden spoons (in case children do not like to get their hands messy)

Aprons

Jelly

Water

Sand

Flour

Water-spray bottle

Ice cubes

Hot-water bottle filled with warm water

Visuals of wet, dry, sticky, damp, cold and hot

MAIN

- Prior to the lesson, place each of the different materials in single bowls and place in the centre of the table.

- Introduce the children to each of the items: ask them if they can name it, and if they can't, then adult to name the item.

- Using one of the visuals (such as 'wet') ask a child to identify a bowl that contains something wet. Repeat with all the children in the group.

- Let the children explore all the materials. Then add items such as the water-spray bottle and the hot-water bottle.

- See if the children can make something sticky, or if they can turn the wet flour dry.

- Take photos as you work through this lesson to use later.

PLENARY

Count the children down '5, 4, 3, 2, 1, finished'. Ask all the children to go and wash their hands.

CONSOLIDATION ACTIVITIES

Print out the photos that you took of the lesson. Place these all on a large piece of paper. Present the visual labels of wet, sticky, dry, etc. Ask the children to find a picture of them exploring something to match the label. Give them glue and ask them to stick this down. Repeat to create a poster of different textures and the changes that materials went through.

28. Power Up

Learning Objective

Developing

Pupils identify some applications that use electricity.

Additional Skills

Visual: selecting favoured toy.

Fine motor: inserting batteries.

Social communication: negotiating resources with other children.

Resources

Cause and effect toys that need batteries

Cause and effect toys with wind-up mechanism

Large box

Batteries for the toys

Screwdriver set

MAIN

- Invite the children to sit around the table. Present the box with the cause and effect toys and the box with the batteries.

- Show a battery and ask if any of the children know what it is called.

- Choose a toy from the box and press 'go' (it won't work); ask the children what is wrong.

- They are likely to tell you it needs batteries, or take the battery from you and try and fix it.

- Show them a toy that does not require batteries. Let the children explore that there is nowhere for the battery to go.

- Place the toys and batteries on the table and allow the children to choose toys and fix them. Close adult supervision is needed when inserting batteries into the toys.

PLENARY

Count down the children and ask someone to put a toy in the box that has batteries and uses electricity. Repeat until all the toys are put away.

CONSOLIDATION ACTIVITIES

When the toys run out of batteries in the class, leave them out for the children to see if they can generalise the skill and seek support to add batteries.

29. So Noisy!

Learning Objective

Developing

Pupils sort materials according to a single criterion when the contrast is obvious.

Additional Skills

Visual: selecting item.

Fine motor skills: manipulating items to make a noise.

Social communication: negotiating resources with other children.

Auditory: seeks something that makes a noise.

Resources

LEGO® brick

Selection of musical instruments

Saucepan and wooden spoon

Water bottle with lentils (shaker)

Pan lids

MAIN

- The criterion is 'something that makes a noise'. This activity is graded so that it gets more challenging for the children.

- Start by placing three musical instruments and a LEGO brick on a tray. Ask the children to choose something that makes a noise.

- For the second turn, place two different instruments, the LEGO brick and a saucepan and wooden spoon on the tray.

- Ask the children to find something that makes a noise. If no one chooses the saucepan and spoon, turn it over and bang it like a drum with the spoon and say 'Noisy!'

- For the final turn place the saucepan and spoon, a bottle filled with lentils, two pan lids and any other items in the class that will make a noise.

- Create a group band, put a piece of music on and everyone plays his or her 'instrument'.

PLENARY

Adult does a beat; the children copy. A child does a beat; rest of the class copy as child puts instrument away. Keep going until everything is back in the box.

CONSOLIDATION ACTIVITIES

Encourage children to sort items in the class; let them help with washing the art materials and sorting brushes and pots, etc.

30. Little Red Hen Baking

Learning Objective

Developing

Pupils closely observe the changes that occur.

Additional Skills

Tactile: exploring different textures.

Attention: following simple instructions to complete a task.

Social communication: working as part of a small group.

Resources

A copy of the story 'The Little Red Hen' (ideally one for each child or per pair)

Seeds for scattering

Soil in a tray/tub

Straws (to represent the corn stalks)

Scissors

Flour

Water

Bowls

Basic bread recipe

Access to an oven

Tablet/camera

MAIN

• Support the children to sit at the table ready to learn. Explain that today we are going to help the little red hen make bread!

• Encourage the child to open the book and all together read the story. On each page recreate the little red hen's actions; e.g. scatter the seeds in the soil, cut the straws to represent cutting the corn, make and bake the bread, and enjoy eating the bread all together!

• At each step encourage the children to notice the changes that occur; i.e. the seeds grow into the corn, and the flour and water become the bread.

• Take photos of the children as they take part in the story.

PLENARY

After eating the bread that has been made encourage the children to discuss the changes that occurred; e.g. before the corn was small, then it was tall; the flour was wet, then dry when it was bread, etc.

CONSOLIDATION ACTIVITIES

Use the photos that were taken during the story to make a class story about growing seeds and baking bread. Read the story with the children at different times and encourage them to notice the changes that occur with e.g. the seeds, the flour and water. When repeating this lesson begin to ask children what they think will happen; e.g. the seeds will grow, the flour and water will be bread. Use symbols to support this process.

30. Little Red Hen Baking *cont.*

Teaching note: we sometimes had pre-made bread for this activity, which smelled amazing while it was warming in the oven while reading the story! However, be aware that if children become used to their ingredients being cooked immediately they may find it difficult to wait for food to be baked in the future!

31. Butter Me Up!

Learning Objective

Developing

Pupils closely observe the changes that occur.

Additional Skills

Gross motor: shaking a plastic bottle.

Visual: observing physical change from liquid to solid.

Social communication: commenting on the change.

Resources

Clear plastic bottles (preferably with a wide rim)

Whipping cream/thick double cream

Simple instruction sheet (can be made using a symbol-writing machine)

Pre-made butter

Laminated 'cream' and 'butter' symbols

A4 sheet of paper with two columns, one labelled 'before' the other 'after'

MAIN

- Support a small group to sit in a semicircle or at the table ready to learn.

- Explain that today we are going to make butter. Show the children the pre-made butter and encourage them to explore and taste it.

- Show the children the cream and explain that it is 'liquid'; ask what they think will happen when we shake it (support to answer using symbols, speech or sign).

- Model for the children the instructions as follows:

  Pour cream into the bottle; shake the bottle for a long time; squeeze out the butter; eat the butter!

- Support the children to conduct the experiment – it can take 10 to 15 minutes for the cream to turn into butter so taking turns shaking the bottle is a good idea!

- When the cream has turned into butter, squeeze it out and taste with fresh bread (maybe from the Little Red Hen Baking lesson!).

PLENARY

Show the children the cream symbol and the butter symbol, support them to sort the symbols into the 'before' and 'after' columns on the A4 piece of paper. Use language such as 'Before the experiment the cream was liquid; after it became butter, it is solid.'

CONSOLIDATION ACTIVITIES

Support the child to closely observe a range of liquid-to-solid changes in their play or in other lessons e.g. water to ice, cornflour when water added.

32. Berry Nice

Learning Objective

Developing

Pupils begin to make generalisations, connections and predictions from regular experience.

Additional Skills

Fine motor: accurately pouring liquid into a mould.

Tactile: experiencing different temperatures and textures.

Communication: following simple instructions.

Resources

Different berries e.g. raspberries, blackberries, blueberries.

Ice lolly moulds

Jugs (one per child or pair)

Access to a freezer

Water

Simple instructions sheet (using a symbol-writer if available)

A4 sheet divided into two with 'before' and 'after' in each column

MAIN

- Support the children to sit at the table ready to learn. Adult explains that when water gets really cold it freezes. We can make water really cold by putting it in the freezer (using visual supports such as pictures will help with this explanation).

- Adult explains that today we are going to make ice-lollies. Adult models following the instructions as follows:

  Squash the berries into the lolly mould; pour water in the mould; take a picture; place the mould in the freezer; in the morning take lollies out of the freezer; take a picture; eat the lollies!

- Support the children to explore the berries and follow the instructions to place the lolly moulds into the freezer.

- Ask them, what do they think will happen to the water? Will it be cold or hot? Will it be frozen or unfrozen? Record their guesses (either verbal or choosing symbols) by writing them down or sticking the symbol they chose or indicated onto a piece of paper.

- In the morning support the children to go to the freezer and take out the lolly moulds. Explore the lollies and discuss their predictions: Was the water hot or cold? Frozen or unfrozen?

PLENARY

Print out the pictures the children took as indicated in the instructions. Support them to sort the photos into the 'before' and 'after' columns to indicate they have noticed the change in materials.

32. Berry Nice *cont.*

Camera/tablet

Laminate hot/cold, frozen/unfrozen symbols

CONSOLIDATION ACTIVITIES

Repeat this activity and freeze water for other purposes e.g. hiding small world figures in ice, making a frozen scene in winter. Each time support the children to make a prediction about what will happen to the water when it goes in the freezer, and support them to use symbols or speech to discuss what happened after the experiment.

33. Light or Sound Chase

Learning Objective

Developing

Pupils show that they know some sources of sound and light.

Additional Skills

Communication: listening and responding to simple instructions.

Social communication: playing a game as part of a small group.

Fine and gross motor: activating the light or sound device.

Resources

A range of light sources e.g. torch, OHP/light box, light switch, disco ball light

A range of sound sources e.g. drums, rainsticks, CD player, microphone

A large space such as the hall or cleared classroom

Laminated light and sound symbols

MAIN

- In a small group show the children the light and sound sources and sort them using the 'light' and 'sound' symbols.

- Encourage the children to explore the resources and support them to operate the devices.

- In the large space, adult places the light and sound sources in different areas.

- Ask the children to stand in a small group at the front of the large space. Explain that when the adult says 'light' and shows the light symbol the children have to run around the room, find a light source and turn it on. If the adult says 'sound' and shows the sound symbol the children have to run around the room, find a sound source and again turn it on.

- Play the game encouraging the children to support each other to find and operate the different light and sound sources.

PLENARY

At the end of the lesson ask the children to tidy up and bring all the resources back to the front of the room. Support the children to sort the resources into the 'light' and 'sound' symbols.

CONSOLIDATION ACTIVITIES

Across the day ask the child to operate light and sound devices: e.g. when walking into a room ask them to turn the lights on; when listening to music at the end of the day ask them to turn on the CD player/computer speakers.

34. Bug Hunt

Learning Objective

Developing

Pupils begin to make generalisations, connections and predictions from regular experience.

Additional Skills

Kinaesthetic: moving around different areas of the school and playground.

Fine motor: using different equipment to collect insects.

Communication: indicating where to hunt for insects.

Resources

Books/websites/songs about insects and where they might be found

'Bug-hunting kits' – clear tubs, magnifying glasses, spade

Large 'plan' of school playground/where you are going to hunt for mini-beasts (this can be hand-drawn)

Symbols of mini-beasts likely to be found e.g. spiders, worms, snails,

Plastic, small world versions of mini-beasts

Glue sticks

MAIN

• As a group, talk about different places you might be able to find mini-beasts. Look at books and stories to prompt children's ideas.

• Explain that we are going to go on a hunt for mini-beasts! Model for the children how to use the 'bug hunter' kits using the small world versions of mini-beasts.

• Look at the plan of the school playground/where you are going to hunt for insects and support the children to indicate where we might find the mini-beasts e.g. by the trees, in the mud. Make a note of these on the plan by e.g. putting a tick next to the place the children indicate.

• Go on a bug hunt around the school grounds, following your plan as to where to look. Support the children to glue a symbol onto the plan where the mini-beast was found in that area.

PLENARY

Back in the classroom look again at the plan and comment on where the mini-beasts were found and which ones they were. Did the children choose the right places to hunt? Were their predictions correct? Explore the found mini-beasts by making drawings, taking photos, etc. Return the mini-beasts to outside, after the lesson has finished.

CONSOLIDATION ACTIVITIES

Repeat this lesson several times, each time making a new plan so that the children have the opportunity to learn from, and build on, previous experiences. When playing outside encourage adults to ask children about where they find mini-beasts.

35. Wind It Up!

Learning Objective

Developing

Pupils sort materials according to a single criterion where the contrast is obvious.

Additional Skills

Fine motor: winding up the toys.

Social communication: working as part of a pair.

Communication: commenting on the actions of the wind-up toy.

Resources

A range of wind-up toys that go at different speeds

Two trays

Laminated 'fast' and 'slow' symbols

Masking tape

MAIN

- Support the child to choose a partner to work with.

- Ask the children to stand at one end of a table and use masking tape to mark out a 'finish line' not too far up the table.

- Adult shows the children two of the wind-up toys and asks the children to guess which one is fast and which one is slow. Adult models winding up a fast one and a slow one, and racing them against each other. Cheer them on! At the end support the children to sort them into the fast and slow symbols.

- Support the children to choose wind-up toys, guess which one is fast and which one is slow, wind them up, race against each other and then sort them into the 'fast' and 'slow' symbols at the end of the race.

PLENARY

Once all the wind-up toys have raced, look at the two trays and encourage the children to comment on the fast and slow wind-up toys. Encourage them to think about how one might have been fast and one might have been slow e.g. one might have jumped and one might have legs.

CONSOLIDATION ACTIVITIES

Use the wind-up toys in different circumstances and see if the results are still the same e.g. over a rough surface or down a slope.

36. Up the Beanstalk

Learning Objective

Developing

Pupils understand the scientific use of some simple vocabulary.

Additional Skills

Visual: noticing changes.

Fine motor: holding something small.

Communication: making a prediction.

Resources

Beans planted before lesson

'Jack and the Beanstalk' story

Beans

Pots

Soil/cotton wool

MAIN

- Well in advance of this lesson (ideally a week) plant a bean and another one a few days before the lesson.

- Start the lesson by reading a simple version of Jack and the Beanstalk.

- Give each child a bean to look at. Be careful to avoid ingestion – close adult supervision is needed.

- Tell the children they are going to grow their own beanstalk. Show them the ones that you have planted, which should have started to grow.

- Ask each child to draw a picture or take a photo of their bean, and make a prediction using the starter 'I think that…'

- Provide pots, soil, cotton wool and water for the children to plant their beans.

PLENARY

Ask each of the children to write their name on their pot and place it on the window sill.

CONSOLIDATION ACTIVITIES

Each day check on the progress of the bean. If the soil or cotton wool is dry, then add water, etc. Talk to the children about what they think is happening.

37. Cress Head

Learning Objective

Developing

Pupils can communicate related ideas and observations using simple phrases.

Additional Skills

Visual: noticing changes.

Fine motor: holding something small.

Communication: making a prediction.

Resources

Beans planted in previous lesson

Cress

Beans

Pots

Soil/cotton wool

MAIN

• Carry out this lesson after 'Up the Beanstalk' so that you have a comparison.

• Show the children cress seeds and beans from the previous lesson. Ask them to compare and make observations (small/big, lots/few, etc.).

• Plant some of the cress in soil and some in cotton wool. Add water to each of the pots.

• Take photos of the pots and ask the children to record the process.

PLENARY

Ask each of the children to write their name on their pot and place it on the window sill.

CONSOLIDATION ACTIVITIES

After four days, compare the cress seeds and the beans. Which is growing faster? Which has more plants? Which is growing taller? Ask the children to record their observations.

38. Film Stars

Learning Objective

Developing

Pupils make simple records of their findings.

Additional Skills

Visual: keeping the focus on the central item being recorded.

Gross motor: holding a recording device still.

Communication: talking to a wider audience.

Resources

Pictures and photos from previous growing lessons

Strips of white card

Pens

Tablet for each child

MAIN

- Using the photos, drawings and written records from the two previous planting lessons (beans and cress), the children will make a short video of their findings.

- The children need to place their drawings in order and then label each of the stages. This can be with scientific terminology if the child is able; if not then use language such as 'first, next, then, last'.

- Using a tablet device, support the child to record their own sequence. They can either film themselves talking about it, take pictures and use a film-editing app, or record a silent film.

- If possible, encourage the children to narrate their findings.

PLENARY

Ask each child to save their work, close the tablets and put them back on the docking station.

CONSOLIDATION ACTIVITIES

During the next communication or English lesson, have each child present their video to the class. Encourage the other children to ask questions about the video that they have seen.

39. Louder

Learning Objective

Developing

Pupils can demonstrate simple properties of sound.

Additional Skills

Fine motor: controlling tablet device.

Visual: noticing visual supports.

Communication: following instructions.

Resources

Visuals of loud and quiet

Drum for each child

Toy microphone for each child

Tablet for each child

MAIN

- All sit around a table and show the children a visual of loud and quiet. Ask them to model being loud and quiet by showing them the visuals. Then show a 'stop' visual and wait for each child to stop. Explain that they are going to use different equipment to make loud and quiet sounds.

- Provide each child with a drum; show the 'loud' and 'quiet' visuals repeatedly and then the 'stop' visual.

- Next, provide each child with a toy microphone and repeat as with the drum.

- Finally provide a tablet to each child and show them the visuals.

PLENARY

Ask the children to place the equipment in the box. Adult takes a tablet, shows the visual of 'quiet' and plays some quiet music for the final 3 minutes of the session.

CONSOLIDATION ACTIVITIES

Place loud and quiet visuals in the music box so that the children can explore the volume. If the class are getting a little noisy, show them the loud visual and then replace it with the quiet visual to support them controlling their volume in class.

40. States of Matter

Learning Objective

Developing

Pupils understand the scientific use of simple vocabulary.

Additional Skills

Fine motor: exploring textures and states.

Visual: noticing features of items.

Social interaction: working with a small group, asking for a turn.

Resources

Balloons

Air pump

Party blowers

Cars

LEGO®

Water

Juice

Baby oil

Visuals of 'solid', 'liquid' and 'gas'

MAIN

- Place three visuals in front of the children: 'solid', 'liquid' and 'gas'.

- Model to the children examples of each type. This could be a LEGO brick and a jug of water, and blowing and releasing a balloon.

- Allow the children time to explore all of the items that you have placed on the table. Adults to model naming the property of the item as the children explore.

- Take photos during the activity and record the children's language and comments through the exploration.

PLENARY

Ask the children to place the equipment in the box. Count down '5, 4, 3, 2, 1, finished'.

CONSOLIDATION ACTIVITIES

On the next really cold day, go outside and look at a frozen puddle and talk to the children about it being a solid, liquid or gas. Could they use anything to turn it back to a liquid?

41. Put It Up

Learning Objective

Developing

Pupils can make simple records of their findings.

Additional Skills

Fine motor: writing and positioning work.

Communication: working with others on shared project.

Auditory: following verbal instructions.

Resources

Materials from the 'States of Matter' lesson

Photos and voice clips from 'States of Matter' lesson

Backing paper and boarders

Glue/stapler

Visuals of 'solid', 'liquid' and 'gas'

Paper and pens

MAIN

- Following on from the 'States of Matter' lesson, have all the photos and voice clips ready to share with the children.

- Place the photos on the table and play the voice clips.

- Present the same objects from the lesson again and offer the children visuals of 'solid', 'liquid' and 'gas' and ask them to label the items.

- Tell the children that they need to make a display; give them time and space to organise the items, the visuals and the photos.

- Adults can model using photos of objects or adding Velcro to real objects to cover the board.

- Remind the children to label their work.

PLENARY

Once the children are happy with the arrangement, put the display together on the board. Let the children choose the coloured paper and borders that they want to use.

CONSOLIDATION ACTIVITIES

Place some spare labels next to the display so that if the children come across a material and correctly identify its property, they can add it to the display board.

42. Vroom Vroom

Learning Objective

Developing

Pupils can demonstrate simple properties of movement.

Additional Skills

Fine motor: winding-up toys.

Communication: working with others and following instructions.

Resources

Toy cars

Wind-up toys

Pull and go toys

Masking tape

Marker pen

MAIN

- All sit around a table and place the basket of toys in the middle. Allow the children to explore how they make them move.

- Place masking tape in two lines on the floor about 1 metre apart. Write start and finish with the children on the lines.

- Everyone in the group chooses their favourite toy and lines them up on the start line.

- The adult calls 'Ready, steady, go!' and the toys race.

- A tally chart is made for the race, listing toys rather than children.

- All swap and try again. Repeat.

PLENARY

Sitting together, count up the tally scores and see which toy won. Starting in last place, ask the children to place the toys one by one in the box.

CONSOLIDATION ACTIVITIES

This activity, now it has been modelled, can be placed as a free choosing time game.

43. Volcanoes!

Learning Objective

Developing

Pupils understand the scientific use of some simple vocabulary and can communicate related ideas and observations using simple phrases.

Additional Skills

Communication: following/giving simple instructions.

Social communication: communicating to others what is happening.

Fine motor: pouring ingredients to conduct the experiment.

Resources

Interactive whiteboard (IWB)

Clear plastic bottles in a range of sizes and shapes

Vinegar

Bicarbonate of soda

Food colouring (optional)

Trays/washing up bowls

Funnel

Spoon

Pipettes

Camera/tablet

MAIN

- In a small group support the children to sit at the table ready to learn.

- Explain that today we are going to experiment making volcanoes!

- Adult shows the children the equipment and verbally labels each item.

- Adult models using the equipment to conduct the experiment using the following instructions:

- Place bottle in tray; pour in vinegar (funnel can be used); pour in food colouring (if using) (pipette can be used); put in bicarbonate of soda; shake the bottle. What happens?

- Support the children to experiment using the equipment and the ingredients. What happens if a smaller/bigger bottle is used? Can you change the colour of the lava? What happens if only a little bit of vinegar is used? And so on.

- Ask simple questions throughout the experiment e.g. what will happen? Support child to answer using speech/symbols/sign.

- Adults to take photos of each step of the experiment, or support the children to take photos of their classmates conducting the experiment.

PLENARY

Upload the photos onto the IWB and look at them all together. Encourage the child to comment on what was happening, the changes that occurred and the use of different equipment. Make the photos into a book to share as a class or use the photos with the child to sequence the experiment or plan the next experiment.

43. Volcanoes! *cont.*

Simple instructions
(can be written using a
symbol-writing program)

Laminated symbols
to support the child
to comment e.g. 'big',
'grows', 'explodes',
colour symbols, 'smells
good', 'bad', 'fast', 'slow'

CONSOLIDATION ACTIVITIES

Place this lesson within a topic on the planet earth
or volcanoes. Extend the learning through looking
at books/websites and making art/stories. Build
the volcano experiment into play; e.g. put all the
ingredients and equipment outside for the children to
independently explore. Make a papier-mâché volcano
scene and conduct the experiment within that. All the
while develop the child's scientific use of vocabulary;
e.g. lava is hot when it comes out of the volcano and
then it gets cold: the lava flows fast then slows down.

44. Round and Round the Playground

Learning Objective

Developing

Pupils can demonstrate the simple properties of sound and movement.

Additional Skills

Kinaesthetic: moving fast and slow.

Gross motor: using and operating playground equipment.

Auditory: listening for changes in sound and speed of heart rate.

Resources

Stethoscopes

A4 laminated 'stop' and 'go', 'fast' and 'slow' symbols

Smaller laminated 'fast' and 'slow' symbols

A4 recording sheet titled 'Experiment' with three columns labelled 'before', 'after' and 'results', and rows for 'running fast', 'climbing fast', 'walking slow'

Access to playground (or if necessary PE) equipment

Whiteboards and pens

MAIN

- Adult supports the children to sit in a semicircle in the playground.

- Adult explains that today we are going to listen to our heartbeats to see if they are going fast or slow. We will then do some exercises and listen to our heartbeats again to see if they are fast or slow.

- Ask the children 'Do you think your heartbeat is fast or slow?'

- Support the children to add a 'fast' or 'slow' symbol to the 'guess' recording sheet in the 'before' column.

- Support the children to work in pairs to use the stethoscope to listen to their heartbeats. If possible use a whiteboard and pen to tally the beats as they hear them.

- Ask the children to guess if their heartbeats will be fast or slow after running fast, by placing a laminated 'fast' or 'slow' symbol on the 'guess' recording sheet in the 'after' column.

- Next, adult uses the large 'fast' symbol to ask the children to run fast around the playground. After a short time e.g. 1 minute of running, adult counts down '5, 4, 3, 2, 1, running finished'. Support the children to sit back down in the semicircle and listen to their heartbeats again.

- Adult asks, 'Are your hearts beating fast or slow after running?' Support the children to choose a smaller laminated 'fast' or 'slow' symbol and then place it in the 'results' column in the row 'running fast'.

- Repeat this process for 'climbing fast' and 'walking slow'.

44. Round and Round... *cont.*

PLENARY

Support the children to sit back in the semicircle and look at the recording sheet together. Look at how many times guesses were right or wrong; comment on when heartbeat was fastest or slowest.

CONSOLIDATION ACTIVITIES

When the activity is repeated extend the guessing and recording aspect by accessing different PE equipment at different speeds or in different ways: e.g. guess a fast or slow heartbeat before sitting on the roundabout, listen afterwards and record; guess a fast or slow heartbeat before pushing the roundabout, listen afterwards and record. Begin to look at results across different equipment and different activities to make more informed predictions.

45. Frolicking Fruit

Learning Objective

Developing

Pupils make simple recordings of their findings.

Additional Skills

Attention: attending to and partaking in the lesson for 15 to 20 minutes.

Communication: commenting on experiment.

Visual: watching the result of their actions.

Resources

Range of different fruits such as raisins, berries, thin strips of apple

Bicarbonate of soda

Water

White vinegar

Clear bottle/jar/cup

A4 piece of paper with a table divided into three columns ('move', 'not move' and 'results') and with a row for each fruit that will be used in the experiment

Small 'move' and 'don't move' symbols

MAIN

- To set up the experiment prepare the fruit by placing the fruit in a bowl with some water and adding teaspoons of bicarbonate of soda: if all the bicarbonate of soda dissolves add a little more until there a some grains left. Leave this for about 15 minutes. Take the fruit out of the solution before the experiment.

- Support the children to sit at the table ready to learn.

- Adult shows the children the fruit and selects one e.g. a blueberry. Adult models making a guess as to whether or not the fruit will move when placed in the vinegar by making a mark in either the 'move' or 'not move' column on the recording sheet.

- Adult fills the transparent bottle/jar/cup with vinegar, places in the fruit and then everyone watches to see what happens.

- If it moves, adult makes a mark to indicate this in the results column e.g. a tick, smiley face, a 'move' symbol. If it doesn't move, adult makes a mark to indicate this in the results column e.g. a cross, sad face, a 'don't move' symbol.

- Support the children to explore and experiment by first very briefly soaking their chosen fruit in water and bicarbonate of soda and then dropping in the vinegar, observing the results of their actions and then recording the results.

- Support the child to choose how they would like to record their findings e.g. ticks/crosses/faces/symbols.

PLENARY

Look at the children's results and compare them. Did the fruit do what we expected? Which ones moved the best? Did we all get the same results?

45. Frolicking Fruit *cont.*

CONSOLIDATION ACTIVITIES

Repeat this experiment with different fruits and other items such as seeds, and use the recording-sheet template each time. After conducting the experiment several times, look at all the results recordings together and decide which fruits/seeds move the best.

46. Filter Flowers

Learning Objective

Developing

Pupils begin to make suggestions for planning and evaluating their work.

Additional Skills

Fine motor: making pre-writing shapes with a pen.

Visual: observing the results of their own actions.

Communication: making simple comparisons between their work and real flowers.

Resources

Coffee filters (large round ones work well)

Clear plastic cups (or jars, but be aware of using glass)

Water

A range of real flowers in various colours e.g. roses, daisies, sunflowers

A range of coloured felt-tip pens (that match the colours of the flowers)

Laminated colour symbols

MAIN

- Support the children to sit at the table ready to learn.

- Present each flower to the children and name it. Encourage the children to explore and comment on the flowers e.g. naming the colour of the flower.

- Adult models choosing a colour from the choosing board, e.g. red, and placing it on the sentence strip.

- Adult models finding a flower that matches the colour and choosing that symbol from the choosing board, e.g. rose, and placing it on the sentence strip to make 'red rose'.

- Adult models finding a red pen from a choice of coloured felt-tip pens, making a circle on the filter paper (around the bottom of the filter paper below the crinkly folds) and then folding the filter paper into a small triangle.

- Adult models placing the filter paper with the nose of the triangle into the water in the cup and watches what happens.

- Once all the colour has moved up the paper, open it out and show the children the flower that has been made.

- Support the children to plan for their own flower experiments by choosing a colour and a matching flower, and then a matching coloured pen.

- Encourage the children to be as independent as possible in conducting the experiment, including how much water to add to the transparent cup, what shapes to make on the coffee filter, and how many times to fold the paper.

- Repeat several times so that the child becomes as independent as possible in planning and conducting the experiment.

46. Filter Flowers *cont.*

Laminated flower symbols

Choosing board

Laminated sentence strip

PLENARY

Look at all the flowers that have been made by the child. Encourage them to match them to their chosen flower and evaluate them by commenting on whether they like or don't like their flowers using speech/sign/symbols. Support the child to say why they like or don't like their flowers; e.g. they look the same/different, too big/small.

CONSOLIDATION ACTIVITIES

Support the child to decide what to do with their flowers: e.g. to make a display for science; make them into cards for parents or carers; make them into invites for a party.

Teaching note: when repeating this lesson, reduce adult modelling so that the child becomes more independent in planning for their own experiment.

47. Puzzle Piece Rescue

Learning Objective

Developing

Pupils begin to make suggestions for planning and evaluating their work.

Additional Skills

Social communication: sharing ideas with a partner.

Fine motor: using different equipment to conduct experiment.

Resources

An inset puzzle (pieces need to be wood-based not paper-based)

Water

Trays

Bicarbonate of soda

Vinegar

Salt

Water-spray bottle

Tools for removing items from ice e.g. spade, plastic hammer/chisel

Laminated symbols for vinegar, salt and water

MAIN

- To set up this experiment place puzzle pieces in a mould such as a small bowl; pour over the top a mixture of water and bicarbonate of soda (about two tablespoons of bicarbonate of soda to half a cup of water); and place in the freezer overnight. Add food colouring if wanted. Remove the frozen puzzle pieces from the moulds just before starting the lesson.

- Support the children to sit in pairs at the table ready to learn.

- Show the children the empty puzzle board and say 'Oh no! Our puzzle is missing all the pieces!' Show the children the frozen moulds with the puzzle pieces and ask, 'How can we get them out?'

- Give each pair a tray, a recording sheet and a frozen mould.

- Present the children with the options for rescuing the puzzle pieces – the vinegar, salt, water, tools for removing items from ice e.g. spade, plastic hammer/chisel.

- Explain that they can try each one and need to record if it works by using a tick/cross/smiley/sad face in the box next to each picture of the option.

- Support the child to plan for the experiment by choosing one of the options from the choosing board e.g. the water spray.

- Support the child to experiment; e.g. use the 'water spray' and then record if it melted the ice or not. Repeat for all the different options.

47. Puzzle Piece Rescue *cont.*

Choosing board

A recording sheet with symbols of vinegar, salt, water, tools for removing items from ice (e.g. spade, plastic hammer/chisel) in rows down one side of the paper and a space next to them for recording results

Food colouring (optional)

PLENARY

Once all the puzzle pieces are released from the ice, support the children to work together to complete the puzzle. Look at all of the results and evaluate what happened when each option was used e.g. the vinegar made it fizz!

CONSOLIDATION ACTIVITIES

Set up the same experiment but in different ways so different methods to melt the ice will work: e.g. freeze in only water so that salt might work; freeze the puzzle piece in vinegar so adding bicarbonate of soda will work.

Support the children to design the experiment for their friends so that one half of the group freeze the puzzle piece/object (deciding on what to use), and the other half have to investigate what will rescue the puzzle piece/object.

Teaching note: other items can be frozen in the mixture depending on child's interest e.g. LEGO®, magnetic alphabet letters.

48. Let's Build a Snowman!

Learning Objective

Developing

Pupils understand the scientific use of some simple vocabulary and can communicate related ideas and observations using simple phrases.

Additional Skills

Tactile: exploring different textures.

Communication: commenting on experiment.

Fine motor: use of equipment such as pipette to develop pincer grip.

Resources

Shaving foam

Bicarbonate of soda

Orange food colouring

Black/blue food colouring

Small bowls

Pipettes

Trays

Camera/table

Laminated simple instructions (a symbol program can be used for this)

MAIN

- Adult explains that today we are going to build a snowman! First we have to make the snow.
- Adult models pouring bicarbonate of soda into a tray and then squeezing in the shaving foam.
- Adult models mixing the two together to make 'snow'. Adult then uses the mixture to build a snowman; i.e. one big ball, one small ball, with small ball on top of big ball.
- Adult then models using the pipette to use the black food colouring to make 'eyes' and 'mouth' and orange food colouring to make 'nose' to complete the snowman! Adult models taking a picture of the snowman.
- Support the child to follow the simple instructions to make the snow and build their own snowman. Encourage child to make comments as they experiment imitating adult's language e.g. the shaving foam gets big, big/small ball, eyes, nose, mouth, pour, mix, squeeze, soft, smooth.
- When the child has built their snowman, support them to take a photo.

PLENARY

Look at all the photos of the snowmen and encourage children to comment on them: e.g. colour, how many eyes/noses snowmen have, which ones they like/don't like and why.

CONSOLIDATION ACTIVITIES

During other science lessons or in other play, encourage child to use simple scientific vocabulary (e.g. soft, smooth, rough, hard, wet, dry) and to comment on changes (e.g. before, the towel was dry, after swimming it was wet).

49. Shadows

Learning Objective

Developing

Pupils can demonstrate the simple properties of light, sound and movement.

Additional Skills

Visual: recognising body features and changes in light and dark.

Communication: listening and responding to instructions.

Fine motor: operating devices that make light.

Resources

Overhead projector (OHP)

Laminated 'dark' and 'light' symbols

Laminated body part symbols e.g. hand, finger, arm, head, foot, elbow

Choosing board

Torch with different settings

MAIN

- To set up this activity place the OHP opposite a wall that is as blank as possible and preferably by a window with blinds (if not using the classroom lights will be fine). Make the classroom dark so that shadows will be very visible.

- Support the child to come into the dark room. Ask the child 'Is it light or dark in here?' and support them to answer using speech/sign/symbols.

- Turn on the OHP; comment that the light is bright.

- Adult models for the child choosing a body part symbol, e.g. hand, and placing it in front of the OHP light to make a hand shadow.

- Support the child to conduct the experiment by first choosing a body part and then using the light to make a shadow. Support the child to answer questions such as 'Is the shadow dark or light?'

- Extend the experiment by opening the blinds/ turning on the classroom lights. Ask the child 'Now is the classroom light or dark?' and support them to answer using speech/sign/symbols.

- Conduct the shadow experiment again and encourage the child to comment on the changes in the shadows made.

PLENARY

Turn off all the lights in the classroom, turn on the torch to the brightest setting and say 'The light is bright!' Make a shadow and support child to comment on whether shadow is light or dark. Turn the setting of the torch to the lowest and say, 'The light is dim.' Try and make a shadow again and support the child to comment. Encourage the child to explore the torch and the settings making the light 'bright' and 'dim' and noticing the effect on their shadow.

49. Shadows *cont.*

CONSOLIDATION ACTIVITIES

Conduct this experiment again but use different objects to cast shadows e.g. pencil, book, dinosaur. Introduce further 'light'/'dark' language such as 'bright' or 'dim'.

50. Shhhh! Don't Wake the Baby

Learning Objective

Securing

Pupils have observed changes in living things.

Additional Skills

Visual: noticing changes.

Fine motor: dressing baby dolls.

Communication: sharing ideas with the group.

Resources

A book about a baby

Picture of a baby, child in class and adult in class

Large piece of paper

Pens

Toy dolls

Baby role-play equipment

MAIN

- Tell the children that this lesson involves comparing a baby to themselves.

- Read a book about a family having a new baby.

- What are all the things that a baby needs help with? Place a picture of a baby on the board and write or draw the things around the baby.

- Now place a picture of one of the class on the board. List all the things that they can do and some of the things they need help with still.

- Finally place a picture of the adult in the room on the board. What are all the things that they can do?

- Ask the children questions about how they learnt to do some of the things they can do now.

- Together, set up a baby clinic role play so that the children can go into role and help the babies learn things that they can now do, such as get dressed and eat.

PLENARY

Count down and ask the children to help put all the babies to bed for the end of the session.

CONSOLIDATION ACTIVITIES

If anyone you know has a baby, ask them to bring him/her to meet the group so that the children can see what it is like and ask the mum or dad questions.

51. Bounce Bounce

Learning Objective

Securing

Pupils make their own observations of movement.

Additional Skills

Visual: being accurate with measuring.

Fine motor: marking the height.

Kinaesthetic: bouncing the balls and catching them when they roll.

Social interaction: collaborative problem-solving.

Resources

Basket

Selection of balls

Tape measures

Clipboards

Paper and pens

MAIN

- Place a basket of balls and a tape measure in the centre of the group.

- Tell the children that the PE teacher has asked them to find the ball that bounces the highest.

- Ask the children to suggest ways to record this. Some suggestions may include working in pairs or sticking the tape measure to the wall.

- Once everyone has a strategy let them start exploring with the balls.

- Adult to model a strategy of putting the tape measure on the wall and working with a partner to drop the ball while the other measures. The adult then records this on a tally sheet with the ball colour and the height it reached.

PLENARY

Ask all the children to place the balls back into the basket and come together as a group. Ask the children which was the ball that bounced the highest. How did they work it out?

CONSOLIDATION ACTIVITIES

Put this activity outside on the playground so that the children can test a range of balls with other peers.

52. Egg to Butterfly

Learning Objective

Securing

Pupils show that they have observed changes in living things.

Additional Skills

Visual: noticing parts of the life-cycle.

Communication: working with others.

Kinaesthetic: moving into phases of cycle.

Resources

Non-fiction book about life-cycle of butterfly

Tablet to play video of life-cycle of butterfly

Visuals of 'egg', 'caterpillar', 'chrysalis' and 'butterfly'

Arrows

Blankets for each child

MAIN

- Read the children a non-fiction book about the life-cycle of a butterfly.

- Ask the children if they know any stories about a caterpillar.

- Show the children a video from the Internet of the life-cycle of a butterfly.

- Using visuals of egg, caterpillar, chrysalis and butterfly create a simple diagram with arrows by giving each of the children a section of the cycle.

- Each part of the cycle has a physical action; adult to model each part of the cycle. The egg is you curling into a ball, and asking everyone to copy. The caterpillar sees you lying flat on the floor and wiggling; again ask everyone to copy. For the chrysalis use a blanket to roll up into and then emerge from the blanket as a butterfly and flap your arms like wings.

- Support the children to each take a turn at acting out the life-cycle.

PLENARY

Film the children doing this together.

CONSOLIDATION ACTIVITIES

Watch the video back and ask the children if they know of any other animals that have a similar life-cycle. Have books and images of frogs available.

53. It Moves

Learning Objective

Securing

Pupils sort materials using simple criteria.

Additional Skills

Visual: recognising key features of items.

Memory: remembering all the items and what is missing.

Kinaesthetic: finding objects in the class.

Resources

Video of moving items and video or pictures of non-moving items

Tray

Moving items

Non-moving items

Sheet

Visuals of 'moving', 'non-moving'

MAIN

- The criteria for this lesson are 'things that move'.
- Ask the children to name something that moves.
- Show them a video from the Internet of something that moves, such as a person walking, a bike or an animal swimming.
- Ask the children to name something that does not move.
- Show them a video or set of pictures of things that do not move such as a post box, a bag, their lunch, a book, etc.
- Place a selection of items that move and don't move onto a tray in front of the children.
- Ask the children to look closely at the items.
- Cover them with a sheet and remove an item. Remove the cover and ask the children to guess what has been removed.
- Once they have guessed, ask them to sort it into the moving or non-moving container. Repeat.

PLENARY

Once the game is over, ask the children to go around the room and find an item that can go into the moving container.

CONSOLIDATION ACTIVITIES

You can play this game with different categories such as hard and soft, living and not living, or light and dark.

54. Recycle Me

Learning Objective

Securing

Pupils can identify some common materials and know about some of their properties.

Additional Skills

Visual: categorising objects.

Fine motor: creating labels.

Kinaesthetic: moving large boxes around.

Social interaction: providing information to others

Resources

Large boxes

Rubbish from lunchtime

Child-friendly recycling video

Paper and pens

MAIN

- Show the children a range of 'rubbish' that you have curated from lunchtime such as paper bags, plastic bottles and crisp packets.

- Ask the children if they know what happens with rubbish.

- Show the children an appropriate waste and recycling video found online.

- As a group, they are going to be setting up a recycling centre to help sort the waste and look after the planet.

- What kind of things did the video say could be recycled?

- Present the groups with large boxes and paper and pens so that they can create labels for the boxes.

PLENARY

Set all the boxes up and look for any rubbish in the class that can be sorted.

CONSOLIDATION ACTIVITIES

Make posters showing people what can be recycled and where they can find the boxes to place their recycling in.

55. Slimey

Learning Objective

Securing

Pupils make some contribution to planning an activity.

Additional Skills

Visual: following pictures or key words.

Fine motor: using utensils to mix and pour.

Kinaesthetic: finding objects in the class.

Communication: being clear what you ask for.

Resources

Child-safe slime recipe (find this online) turned into clear simple instructions

Ingredients as per the recipe, all labelled

Bowls

Spoons

Aprons

MAIN

- Tell the children that they are going to be chemists in this lesson, and it is a chemist's job to mix ingredients to make something new. They need to find the right adult to get the ingredients and equipment they need.

- Provide each child with a set of clear instructions for the slime either in pictures or in simple words.

- Place all the labelled equipment and ingredients on two separate tables in the room with an adult at each one, imagining that they are different 'shops'.

- After each child is wearing an apron, they can begin. Be very literal with how you follow the child's request, and give them the ingredients. If they ask for flour and have not bought a bowl, put a little in their hands to encourage them to think it through.

PLENARY

Once the children have worked through the recipe, it is time to tidy up. Count down and support the children to clear the class.

CONSOLIDATION ACTIVITIES

Have some slime that you made earlier in case the children's slime doesn't work out. Allow them to explore the texture of this and what they can do with it.

56. The Stars in the Sky

Learning Objective

Securing

Pupils show that they have observed changes in events.

Additional Skills

Fine motor: cutting.

Communication: working with others.

Resources

Large pieces of paper

Pens

Scissors

Glue

Poem about night and day

Pictures of stars, sun and moon

Pictures of day activities (swimming, school, bike, etc.)

Pictures of night activities (bed time, fireworks, etc.)

Laminated 'night' and 'day' symbols

MAIN

- Read the children a poem or story about night and day.

- Show the children pictures of stars, the moon and the sun. Ask them when they might see each of these.

- On a large piece of paper, place 'night' and 'day' symbols on separate halves and draw a line down the middle.

- Provide the children with the page of pictures of things that happen at night and during the day. Ask them to sort the pictures and stick them to the grid.

PLENARY

Review the work together. Does everyone agree with where the pictures have been placed? Can anyone think of any other activities that occur?

CONSOLIDATION ACTIVITIES

Ask the children to keep a simple record of what time the sun goes down each day for a week, and share this during the next science lesson.

57. Magnetic Man

Learning Objective

Securing

Pupils identify a range of common materials and know about some of their properties.

Additional Skills

Fine motor: using the magnet and manipulating magnetic items to make a face.

Social communication: working as part of a pair.

Communication: giving and following instructions to/from a classmate.

Resources

Large magnets

A range of magnetic items e.g. large paper clips, metal spoon, keys

A range of obviously non-magnetic items e.g. soft toy, crayon, corn flour

A tray

An A3 body template

Laminated 'magnetic' and 'non-magnetic' symbols

A camera/table

MAIN

- To start this experiment, support the child to choose a partner to work with.

- Place all the items in a large tray, give the children the magnets and encourage them to use the magnets to explore the tray.

- Encourage the children to comment on what is happening when the magnet picks something up, e.g. 'The spoon is magnetic', or if the magnet doesn't pick an object up, e.g. 'The crayon is non-magnetic.' Support the children to sort the magnetic and non-magnetic items into two piles and label with the symbols.

- Mix the items back together in the tray. Model for the children using the magnet to find a magnetic item, e.g. a spoon, and use it to make part of 'Magnetic Man' by placing the spoon onto the leg of the body template.

- Support the children to work together to use the magnets to find magnetic items in the tray to make a 'Magnetic Man' by using these items to fill in the body template.

PLENARY

Support the children to take a photo of their 'Magnetic Man'. When the man is completed ask the children to re-sort the items into two piles using the laminated 'magnetic' and 'non-magnetic' symbols.

CONSOLIDATION ACTIVITIES

When conducting this lesson again, look at the photo the child took of their previous 'Magnetic Man'. Support them to explain to a classmate that the items used to make the man are 'magnetic'. Explore different magnetic and non-magnetic items and build a new 'Magnetic Man' together.

58. Pirate SOS!

Learning Objective

Securing

Pupils sort materials according to simple criteria and communicate their observations of materials in terms of these properties.

Additional Skills

Communication: communicating their observations of the experiment.

Social communication: taking turns and watching a classmate take their turn.

Attention: focusing on and completing an activity as part of a small group for 15 to 20 minutes.

Resources

Water tray

Water

Range of items that float e.g. rubber duck, sweet potato, plastic boat, cork

MAIN

- Support the children to sit in a small group around the water tray, ready to learn.

- Show the children the small world figure and explain that he needs to get across the 'shark-infested water' safely! The children need to find out which objects will float and carry him across, or will sink and won't help him.

- Support the children to put the different items in the water and record their results by placing the picture of the object in either the 'float' or 'sink' column.

- Encourage the children to guess what will happen before the object is placed in the water, and then comment on what happens when the objects are placed in the water.

PLENARY

Ask each child to choose an item that 'floats' and see if that item gets the pirate safely across the water tray. At the end of the experiment support the children to discuss and choose the one item that would be the best item to save the pirate from the shark-infested waters, and comment on why e.g. 'The duck floats and is big enough for the pirate.'

58. Pirate SOS! *cont.*

Range of items that sink e.g. a weight, coin, cloth, pear

Pictures of each of the items

A large sheet of paper or a board divided into two columns labelled 'Float' and 'Sink'

A small world figure such as a pirate

CONSOLIDATION ACTIVITIES

As the child becomes familiar with the lesson, extend the sorting criteria to include other observations such as the objects being wet/dry or small/big. Introduce other items that float or sink which are more ambiguous such as a sponge, and encourage the child to guess and comment on what happens when they are placed in the water tray.

59. It's Raining, It's Pouring

Learning Objective

Securing

Pupils show that they have observed patterns or regular changes in features of objects, living things and events.

Additional Skills

Visual: recognising the difference in quantities of water.

Fine motor: using a pincer grip to record results.

Social communication: working as part of a pair.

Resources

A range of vessels for collecting rainwater e.g. clear plastic bottles/tubs/bowls

Permanent marker pens

Items to make a simple bar chart e.g. strips of paper, large/A3 paper

Wet-weather gear e.g. welly boots, waterproofs, umbrellas

Ruler

MAIN

- Use a simple presentation to show the children the water cycle; i.e. it rains, the sun comes out, the water evaporates and makes clouds, it rains again.

- Explain that we get more rain some times of the year than others. We are going to collect the rainwater and see when it is most rainy and think about why!

- Working in pairs support the children to choose which vessel they will use to collect the rainwater and then think about where they are going to put the vessel: e.g. outside or inside? Under the roof or out in the playground?

- Whenever it rains support the children to go out to their collection vessel and mark a line to indicate how much rain fell.

- Support the children to measure how many centimetres of rain they have collected and record this as a bar graph.

PLENARY

Once the children have recorded rainfall at least three times, look at the bar charts they have created all together and discuss the results: e.g. When did the most rain fall? Why do you think that is? Compare the children's results with each other; for example if one pair kept their rainwater collection vessel under the roof and another out in the playground, why might the results be different?

CONSOLIDATION ACTIVITIES

Use rainwater collected for other experiments (such as 'Cress Head', 'Black Marker Magic' and 'Frolicking Fruit') to support children to generalise their understanding of where water comes from and what it can be used for.

59. It's Raining, It's Pouring *cont.*

Teaching note: the length of time of collection of the rainwater is up to you as the teacher to decide. If the children have the understanding to recall and remember the experiment over time, conducting this experiment over half a term or even a year might be a good idea; if not, doing this over a week or at different times of the year might work best.

60. Black Marker Magic

Learning Objective

Securing

Pupils make some contribution towards planning and evaluation, and to recording their findings.

Additional Skills

Communication: communicating choices to others around them.

Attention: repeating and persisting with an experiment.

Fine motor: using pens and crayons as part of the experiment.

Resources

Coffee filters halved

Non-permanent black marker pens

A range of plastic cups, bottles and bowls

Laminated symbols that match the range of plastic cups, bottles and bowls

Laminated 'more water' and 'less water' symbols

Laminated 'circle' and 'line' symbols

Laminated 'colour' and 'count' symbols

MAIN

- Support the child to sit at the table ready to learn.
- Adult models how to plan for the experiment, i.e. choosing from the range of plastic cups, bottles, bowls, etc. and placing the corresponding symbol next to the number '1' on the instruction sheet. Then adult chooses between the 'more water' and 'less water' symbols and places them beside the number '2'.
- Next, adult models conducting the experiment by taking the coffee filter then choosing between the 'circle' and 'line' symbol and placing that beside the number '3'. Adult then draws, say, a line on the filter paper using the black marker pen.
- Adult pours the chosen amount of water into the chosen receptacle and then places the filter paper as a curve into the receptacle; watch what happens!
- Adult models taking the filter paper out of the receptacle and choosing between the 'colour' and 'count' symbols, and places this symbol next to the number '4'. If 'colour' is chosen use the crayons to record the colours the marker pen released; if 'count' is chosen use the laminated number symbols to indicate how many the marker pen released.
- Next, adult supports child to conduct the experiment by choosing the symbols needed to plan, conduct and evaluate the experiment.

PLENARY

Look at the results of the experiment and discuss what happened e.g. what happened if we used more water? What happened if we drew a circle instead of a line? Discuss the best way to conduct the experiment and take a photo of the instruction sheet.

60. Black Marker Magic *cont.*

All laminated symbols to have soft Velcro on the back

Choosing board

Blank laminated instructions sheet – an A4 piece of paper divided horizontally into three sections titled 'Plan', 'Experiment', 'Evaluate'. In the 'Plan' section have the numbers '1' and '2' down the left-hand side of the page with hard Velcro next to the numbers. In 'Experiment' and 'Evaluate' sections have the numbers '3' and '4' both with hard Velcro next to the numbers.

Water

Jugs

Coloured crayons (to include all the colours of the rainbow)

Laminated number symbols

Camera/tablet

CONSOLIDATION ACTIVITIES

When conducting this experiment again, reduce adult modelling so that the child is taking part in the planing, conducting and evaluating of the experiment with increased independence. Use this method of choosing symbols to begin to plan, conduct and evaluate other experiments.

61. Popping Corn!

Learning Objective

Securing

Pupils sort materials according to simple criteria and communicate their observations of materials in terms of these properties.

Additional Skills

Tactile: tasting, touching and smelling the corn.

Communication: communicating observations to others.

Social communication: waiting a turn as part of a small group.

Resources

Popping corn

Access to a microwave

Laminated 'before' and 'after', 'cooked' and 'not cooked', 'hot' and 'cold', 'hard' and 'soft' symbols

A4 recording sheet titled 'Experiment' with three columns labelled 'before', 'after' and 'results'

MAIN

- Support the children to sit at the table in a small group ready to learn.

- Show the children corn kernels and support them to explore and comment on them e.g. are they hard or soft? Hot or cold? Cooked or not cooked?

- Support the children to record their comments by placing symbols in the 'before' column on the recording sheet.

- Adult explains to the children that the corn is going into the microwave and asks the children what they think the corn will be like 'after'. Support the children to record their guesses on the recording sheet.

- Adult supports a child to come and put the popcorn in the microwave and turn it on.

- Adult takes the popcorn out and asks the children to comment on how it is now. Again support the children to record their answers in the 'results' column on the recording sheet.

- When the popcorn is still warm but no longer too hot to touch, encourage the children to explore the cooked and uncooked popcorn.

- Support the children to sort the popcorn and the corn kernels onto different symbols e.g. hot/cold, soft/hard, cooked/uncooked, before/after.

PLENARY

All together look at the recording sheet and discuss the findings. Were the children's guesses correct? What was the corn like before and after the experiment? Look at the criteria by which the children sorted the cooked and uncooked popcorn; are there any other differences/similarities between the cooked and uncooked popcorn e.g. colour, size, smell, texture?

61. Popping Corn! *cont.*

CONSOLIDATION ACTIVITIES

Repeat this experiment again and this time support the children to choose the criteria and properties by which they will sort the cooked and uncooked popcorn themselves.

62. I Can See a Rainbow!

Learning Objective

Securing

Pupils make their own observations of changes of light that result from actions and can describe the changes when questioned directly.

Additional Skills

Visual: noticing the colours produced by the light through prism.

Communication: communicating their observations to others.

Attention: persisting with the experiment even if it becomes difficult.

Resources

Prisms (acrylic are safest)

Large piece of white paper

Masking tape

Access to a window and a blind

Camera/tablet

Crayons in rainbow colours

Laminated 'light' and 'dark' symbols

MAIN

- To set up this experiment secure the white paper to a window sill using the masking tape.

- Ask the child to come over to the window.

- Adult models looking through the prism, placing it in the light and commenting on what happens.

- Adult then encourages the child to explore the prism in the light by the window, creating and recording rainbows using the crayons on the paper.

- Adult closes the blind to make the room dark.

- Support the child to experiment with the prism again and encourage them to comment e.g. it's dark, no colours, no rainbow.

- Increase the light by pulling up the blind to make it 'brighter' and explore the prisms again; what happens this time?

- Support the child to explore how bright the rainbow is when the room is bright, dim or dark.

PLENARY

At the end of the lesson ask the child to describe what happened when the blind was up, e.g. the light made a rainbow, and then ask them to comment on what happened when the blind came down, e.g. in the dark there was no rainbow.

CONSOLIDATION ACTIVITIES

Support the child to explore prisms in other contexts e.g. out in the playground, on top of the slide or in the tunnel, what happens? What happens on a rainy day?

63. Mini-Beast Sorting

Learning Objective

Securing

Pupils sort materials according to simple criteria and communicate their observations of materials in terms of these properties.

Additional Skills

Visual: recognising similarities and differences.

Communication: explaining their observations and reasoning.

Social communication: listening and responding to the opinions of others.

Resources

Range of small world mini-beasts

Feely bag

A4 laminated symbols for properties of mini-beasts e.g. legs, wings, colours, antennae, no antennae and numbers of legs

MAIN

- To set up this activity place the A4 laminated symbols for the properties of mini-beasts on a table top.

- Bring the children to the table and label each property.

- Adult then models singing the feely bag song to the tune of 'Jingle Bells': 'Feely bag, feely bag, what's inside the feely bag? Put your hand in, feel about, when you're ready pull something out!' and pulling a mini-beast from the bag.

- Adult models observing the mini-beast and then deciding which property to put it on, giving their reason; e.g. if pulled out a grasshopper might decide to put it on the green symbol, as it is green to match the grass and hide from bigger animals.

- Adult supports the children to take it in turns to pull out the mini-beasts and place them on a property symbol and giving a reason why.

- Repeat until all the mini-beasts have been sorted.

PLENARY

Once all the mini-beasts are sorted onto the property symbols stand back and look at them as a group. Adult asks the children to take turns picking a mini-beast and asking if it could go on a different property symbol; e.g. the grasshopper could also go on the antennae symbol, wings symbol and legs symbol. Support the children to make drawings of their chosen mini-beast, being sure to include the property that they sorted them onto.

63. Mini-Beast Sorting *cont.*

CONSOLIDATION ACTIVITIES

This lesson could be conducted in a different way; e.g. all the mini-beasts are on the floor and the children have to race to sort them, and then discuss with their friends why they placed them on a particular property symbol.

Support the children to sort their drawings by particular properties to make a display on the wall.

64. Sunflower Sprint

Learning Objective

Securing

Pupils show that they have observed regular changes in features of living things.

Additional Skills

Fine motor: making drawings as observations.

Communication: commenting on changes.

Attention: sustaining interest and attention on an activity over a long period of time.

Resources

Sunflower seeds

Soil

Plant pots

Water

Water-sprays

Jugs

Paper

Pencils and crayons

MAIN

- With the children discuss a simple presentation about what plants need to grow, i.e. light, water, soil, etc.

- Tell the children we are going to grow our own sunflowers and see whose can grow the quickest and the tallest!

- Support the children to make observations and drawings of the sunflower seeds and to plant them as independently as possible.

- Once the seeds are planted support the children to decide where is best to place their seeds and how best to look after them.

- Over the following weeks encourage the children to remember what plants need to live, i.e. light, water, etc. Ask the children if their plants are getting what they need.

- Make regular observations and drawings of the sunflowers as they start to grow and encourage the children to comment on the changes e.g. getting bigger/taller, colour changes.

PLENARY

Once or twice a week ask the children to bring all of their plants to the group. Whose is tallest? Why might that be? Encourage the children to think about where to put their sunflowers to help them grow the most and to look after them by regularly watering them.

CONSOLIDATION ACTIVITY

Explore plants in different habitats around the school e.g. in the foyer and in the playground. Are they getting what they need to live? Are they taller or shorter than the children's sunflowers? Why might that be?

COMPUTING

65. What's the Weather?

Learning Objective

Emerging

Pupils make selections to generate preferred sounds or images. They know that certain actions produce predictable results.

Additional Skills

Gross motor: operating a switch or selecting a symbol.

Tactile: experiencing different sensory media.

Communication: communicating a choice.

Resources

Four switches with types of weather pre-recorded

Symbols for rain, wind, snow and sun – one placed on each switch

Water-spray

Fan

Shaving foam

Yellow fabric/torn-up yellow tissue paper

Small photos of children and adults in the group

MAIN

- To the tune of 'Frère Jacques' sing the following song: 'What's the weather? What's the weather? I don't know! I don't know! (Child's name) can you tell us? (Child's name) can you tell us?'

- Support the child to select and press a switch with a weather symbol on and celebrate e.g. 'You chose rain!' and spray the group with water-spray.

- Repeat for other children in the group and different weather types: e.g. shaving foam for snow, fan for wind, yellow material/tissue paper for sun.

PLENARY

Show the child a choice of two props and support them to choose the correct switch to press. When they find the correct switch, celebrate by using the prop e.g. placing a small spot of shaving foam in your hands and clapping to make snow.

CONSOLIDATION ACTIVITIES

Play this game outside where the children can make meaningful observations about the weather on the day.

Teaching note: depending on the child's level it might be advisable to start with two choices rather than four initially, and work in small groups of two to three children.

66. Who's on the Farm?

Learning Objective

Emerging

Pupils make selections to communicate meanings.

Additional Skills

Communication: making a choice between four switches/symbols.

Auditory: listening and responding to a familiar song.

Social communication: taking turns in a pair or small group.

Resources

Four switches with names of the farm animals pre-recorded

Laminated cow, pig, duck and sheep symbols (or any other farm animal the child likes) – place a symbol on top of each switch

Small world animals to match symbols

MAIN

• Once the children are seated show them the switches with the animal symbols on top. Press each switch, show the matching small world figure and make the corresponding animal noise.

• All sing 'Old MacDonald' together.

• At the appropriate point in the song ask the child to choose and press a switch. Give the child the small world figure of the animal they chose and everyone make the animal noise together.

• Repeat for the next child in the group.

PLENARY

Present the child with two of the switches. Show the child one of the small world animal figures (this should match one of the switches) and ask them which animal it is. Support the child to answer using the switch and make the noise of the animal.

CONSOLIDATION ACTIVITIES

Switches could also be used to support children to join in with other familiar songs; e.g. during 'Five Little Ducks' the child could select the switch with the correct number corresponding to how many ducks are left in the pond.

Teaching note: depending on the child's level it might be advisable to start with two choices rather than four initially, and work in small groups of two to three children.

67. More Tunes!

Learning Objective

Emerging

Pupils make selections to generate preferred sounds or images. They know that certain actions produce predictable results.

Additional Skills

Communication: indicating wanting 'more' music.

Auditory: listening and responding to music in different ways.

Fine motor: using one finger to operate a piece of equipment.

Resources

CD player

CD of music that is enjoyable and motivating for the child

Switch pre-recorded with the word 'more' and a 'more' symbol on top

MAIN

- Model for the child how to press the 'play' button to start the music on the CD player, and enjoy the music together for a short while, then stop the music.

- Support the child to request 'more' music by either pressing the switch, or signing or vocalising. Praise the child using specific praise e.g. 'Great asking for "more"!'

- Support the child to press the 'play' button for more music and enjoy the music together again.

- Repeat this game of stopping the music, the child requesting 'more' and then pressing the 'play' button.

PLENARY

Do an action that the child enjoys such as clapping or tickling. Abruptly stop the action and support the child to use the switch to request 'more' of the action. Repeat this for various actions.

CONSOLIDATION ACTIVITIES

Use the 'more' switch in other situations across the day e.g. to support the child to ask for 'more' apple at snack time or 'more' tickles during a game.

68. Choose Me!

Learning Objective

Emerging

Pupils make selections to communicate meanings.

Additional Skills

Communication: making a choice between two items.

Gross motor: operating a switch.

Visual: discriminating between two pictures/symbols.

Resources

Two switches

Symbols/pictures of motivating items (toys, snack, etc.)

Corresponding motivating items

MAIN

- To set up the activity, place one symbol/picture of a motivating item on each switch. Pre-record the name of the motivating activity on each switch.

- On the carpet or at the table adult models pressing the switch and then receiving the requested motivating object.

- Show the child the two objects, place them behind the switch and ask the child to choose.

- Support the child to press the switch corresponding to their preferred item.

- Allow the child to explore their chosen item for a short amount of time before counting down '5, 4, 3, 2, 1, (item) has finished'.

- Swap the switches and items around and repeat the activity.

PLENARY

Show the child each of the items and ask them to identify the item by pressing the correct switch.

CONSOLIDATION ACTIVITIES

Support the child to use switches to make choices between two items across the day e.g. between red or blue paint, inside or outside, sand or water play.

Teaching note: when introducing this lesson, offering the child a choice between a motivating and non-motivating item can support meaningful choice-making. As the child becomes more confident discriminating between the switches, introduce a wider range of items and switches.

69. Funny Faces

Learning Objective

Emerging

Pupils make selections to generate preferred images.

Additional Skills

Visual: noticing self and others.

Attention: sharing attention with a familiar adult for a short time.

Auditory: listening and responding to one key word.

Resources

Tablet for each child in the group/class

MAIN

- Ensure that each of the tablet devices are charged prior to the session.

- In one-to-one partnership initially to model how the camera feature works, turn the camera inwards so that the screen and camera are both facing the child, as though it were a mirror.

- Sit with the child and pull some funny faces so that the children can see both of you together.

- Model pressing the camera button using 'photo' as the key word.

- Place the tablet on the table and show the child the photos of themselves and you together.

- Turn it back into camera mode and give the child a chance to explore.

- Adult to move onto working with another child in the group.

- Use the key word 'photo' to encourage the children to press the shutter button on the tablets.

PLENARY

Turn the album feature back on for each child so that they can swipe through their photos.

CONSOLIDATION ACTIVITIES

Print off some of the photos that the children have taken and place them next to a mirror. Can the children make the same face with adults modelling this?

70. Listen and Match

Learning Objective

Emerging

Pupils make selections to communicate meanings.

Additional Skills

Visual: matching picture to sound.

Attention: sharing attention with a familiar adult for a short time.

Auditory: listening to the sounds.

Resources

Tablet or voice-recording device

Printed and laminated cards of each of the sounds you record

MAIN

- Prior to the session use the record function on a tablet or voice recorder to record a range of familiar sounds (kettle, door bell, dog barking, teacher's voice, toilet flush, etc.).

- Create an accompanying picture card of each of the sounds.

- At the start of the activity, show children a visual that says 'listening game'. At this level, the children may not join a session seated at the table: you may need to go to them.

- Play the first sound and wait. Play the same sound two or three times. If any child is showing an interest in the sound, move yourself closer to them and play the sound again.

- Offer the child a choice of two cards – the correct and incorrect.

- If they choose the correct one, give them a high-five, say the sound name and play it again.

- If they choose the second card, say the sound name of that and play the corresponding card.

PLENARY

Offer the children the set of cards and ask them to choose a sound they would like to hear again.

CONSOLIDATION ACTIVITIES

This activity can be placed in the reading area to support listening skills. It can also be carried out as part of Phase 1 phonics where the children identify environmental sounds.

71. Musical Snap

Learning Objective

Emerging

Pupils make selections to communicate meanings.

Additional Skills

Visual: noticing images.

Attention: sharing attention with a familiar adult for a short time.

Auditory: listening to the sounds.

Resources

Whiteboard

PowerPoint presentation of images of instruments

Basket of the instruments (e.g. guitar, triangle, drum, maracas, keyboard, xylophone)

MAIN

- Prior to the session create a PowerPoint of single musical items on each page. Ensure that they are items that you have access to.

- Have the PowerPoint on the computer, or if possible the whiteboard. Place the instruments in a basket in front of the screen.

- Have the first picture of the board and select and make a noise with the accompanying instrument to gain the attention of the children.

- If a child approaches, draw their attention to the screen, point to the basket and say 'choosing'.

- If they choose the corresponding instrument, then keep the picture the same. If they choose a different instrument, then find the matching picture and have this on the screen. Use the key words 'same' and 'different' when the children are choosing and matching.

- Repeat with adults modelling where necessary.

PLENARY

As the instruments go back in the basket, adult to say the name of each and show the corresponding picture.

CONSOLIDATION ACTIVITIES

As the children try this activity a few times, update the PowerPoint so that with each image of an instrument, a piece of music using that instrument is inserted. The children can then use their instrument and accompany the music they are hearing.

72. Stop the Song

Learning Objective

Emerging

Pupils know that certain actions produce predictable results.

Additional Skills

Visual: recognising picture and action.

Attention: sharing attention with a familiar adult for a short time.

Auditory: listening to chosen songs.

Resources

Tablet

Symbols – 'stop', 'go'

Pictures of the songs available

Headphones

MAIN

- Pre-load a selection of the children's favourite nursery rhymes or pop songs to the tablet. Also load some that the children do not like.

- To teach the concept initially, work with children one-to-one. Ask them to choose a song from the pictures. Load the song. Model to the children pressing play and say 'go'. Wait a few moments, press stop and say 'stop'.

- Wait for the child to make an initiation for more. Model this a few times.

- When the child starts to press play and stop themselves, leave the tablet with them so that they can explore this.

- Work around the class. You may need to use headphones with the children who are exploring.

PLENARY

On the class computer, ask a child to choose a favourite song. As a group say 'go' and then 'stop' to control the music.

CONSOLIDATION ACTIVITIES

Add more songs to the selection. This could be stuck to the back of the tablet with Velcro so that the children can make a request to an adult for a song, or an adult can initiate a response from the child by showing them the choices.

73. Swipe It

Learning Objective

Emerging

Pupils use computer programs.

Additional Skills

Visual: recognising picture and action.

Attention: sharing attention with a familiar adult for a short time.

Communication: requesting an item.

Resources

Tablet

Pictures of the apps available

Headphones

MAIN

- Pre-load a selection of art and music apps to the tablet. These can be simple cause and effect apps: i.e. I do something, and then something happens.

- Ask the child to choose an app they would like to play. Show them the corresponding image.

- Give them around three to 5 minutes to explore and manipulate items within the app.

- Say 'finished', take the tablet back and lock it, placing it on the table.

- Wait for the child to make a request for another turn.

- Offer them the pictures so they can choose what they want to play.

- Return the tablet to the child.

- Repeat.

PLENARY

Count the child down '5, 4, 3, 2, 1, tablet has finished'; ask them to turn off the app and lock the tablet and place it back on the teacher's desk.

CONSOLIDATION ACTIVITIES

Once the children have a range of programs that they enjoy, introduce a turn-taking component. Have two children and an adult at a table with a two-minute visual timer. Adult states whose turn it is and turns the timer. When the timer is up, say 'finished' and let the second child have a turn. Repeat. After a while the children will get used to this, and after it is modelled, can be left to negotiate turns for themselves.

74. Spacebar Hit

Learning Objective

Emerging

Pupils use computer programs.

Additional Skills

Visual: tracking a moving image.

Attention: sharing attention with a familiar adult for a short time.

Fine motor skills: pressing spacebar.

Resources

Computer or laptop

Spacebar game

Fabric cut out of keyboard leaving only spacebar visible

Headphones

Sand timer

MAIN

- Prior to the session, speak with your IT coordinator, or use a search engine to find a simple computer program that only requires pressing the spacebar as a cause and effect. This could include popping bubbles or balloons, or pressing the spacebar to have an animal make a noise.

- Set the game up on the class computer or laptops.

- Cover the keyboard with a piece of fabric cut out to the shape of all the other keys, so that only the spacebar remains.

- Start the game. Model to the child pressing the spacebar. If the game has sounds, give the child headphones so that they can engage with the movement and the sound.

- Leave the child to see if they can complete the action of pressing the spacebar.

- Place a five-minute timer with the child, so that they have a visual cue as to when their turn has ended.

PLENARY

Count the child down '5, 4, 3, 2, 1, computer has finished'; ask them to turn off the screen and tuck the chair in.

CONSOLIDATION ACTIVITIES

If you start off with a simple game such as balloon pop, then progress on to a more complex game with the same action such as making a pony jump over a hedge. These can be found if searched for online.

75. The Lion Roars

Learning Objective

Emerging

Pupils make connections between control devices and information on screen.

Additional Skills

Visual: recognising a picture.

Attention: sharing attention with a familiar adult for a short time.

Social communication: waiting for a turn.

Resources

Computer and interactive whiteboard

Presentation of animal pictures and noises

Familiar story about animals

Basket

Soft toy animals from the story

MAIN

- Prior to the lesson, create a PowerPoint presentation that has the pictures of the animals and a sound bite of the noise the animal makes that activates on a click.

- Place the basket of animals in front of the children in the group.

- Start reading the story about the animals.

- As the adult names an animal, ask a child to come and find it from the basket. Then ask another child to press the matching animal on the screen.

- Can everyone make the same noise as the animal?

- Continue reading the story, allowing children to find the animals and make the corresponding sounds.

PLENARY

Ask the children to place their animal back in the basket. They can press the picture so that it makes a noise as it goes back in.

CONSOLIDATION ACTIVITIES

In the book corner, create an animal-themed section with a range of books, the basket of animals and some masks and other props. On switches (such as a Big Mack), place a picture on each one and record the animal noise. Encourage the children to engage with these as they read.

76. I Can Help Too!

Learning Objective

Emerging

Pupils make connections between control devices and information on screen.

Additional Skills

Visual: recognising pictures.

Attention: sharing attention with a familiar adult for a short time.

Social communication: waiting for a turn.

Fine motor skills: manipulating fastenings to put on dressing-up clothes.

Resources

Computer and interactive whiteboard

Presentation of 'people who help us' with four character images (nurse, fireman, police, vet) on the main page, with each picture linking to an image and sounds of the scenario. For example, the fireman links to a picture of a house on fire and the sirens and sounds of water

Props for each of the four characters

MAIN

- Place the resources around the room, including the toy vehicles and the dressing-up props.

- Put the pictures and sounds on the interactive whiteboard.

- Tell the children that today they need to help people. Ask a child to come and choose the character they want to be first.

- As they click the character picture, it will take them to an image and sounds (or video) of the person in action.

- Adult to model finding the resources in the room to get into character.

- Adult support may be needed in the form of prompting and guiding in the first instance.

- When everyone has had a few minutes, ask another child to choose who he or she would like to be. Repeat finding resources that they can use in the scenario.

PLENARY

After everyone has had a turn, adult counts down '5, 4, 3, 2, 1, role play has finished'. Support the children to put all the resources back in the basket.

CONSOLIDATION ACTIVITIES

You could show the children short video clips of a scenario, such as a hospital, and have this set up outside so that the children can then have longer to explore and engage in the play.

77. Greetings!

Learning Objective

Emerging

Pupils use computer programs.

Additional Skills

Visual: recognising own self in a picture.

Fine motor: using controlled finger point to press icon on screen.

Kinaesthetic: moving to come to the interactive whiteboard.

Social communication: taking turns in a small group.

Resources

Interactive whiteboard (IWB)

A pre-made presentation using a program such as PowerPoint with interactive pictures of children in the class, i.e. when you touch the picture an animation happens (preferably one picture per slide per child)

MAIN

- Invite the children to sit in a semicircle around the IWB.
- Everybody sing the 'Hello' song while tapping their legs with their hands chanting, 'Who shall we say hello to? Who shall we say hello to? Oh me, oh my, say helloooo to...' Press the spacebar on the keyboard to reveal the slide with the child's picture.
- Encourage the children to identify themselves by saying 'me' using a switch, speech or sign.
- The chosen child comes up to the IWB, and presses their picture to see the animation.
- Everyone sings the 'Hello' song again and the child presses the spacebar to reveal the next classmate.
- Repeat this until everyone in the group has had a turn.

PLENARY

When everyone has had a turn using the computer program on the IWB, ask how many children are in the class today. Everyone counts the children in the class, then adult chooses one child to come to the IWB to either type the number using the computer keyboard or write the number on the screen using their finger or an IWB pen.

CONSOLIDATION ACTIVITIES

Using the same computer program, create a slide with all the children's photos. When the child needs to choose a friend for an activity or identify who is next, support them to use the IWB to select a picture of their chosen friend.

78. Dance, Dance, Dance!

Learning Objective

Emerging

Pupils make connections between control devices and information on screen.

Additional Skills

Kinaesthetic: moving body in different ways to music.

Gross motor: imitating different dance moves.

Auditory: processing instructions.

Social communication: taking a turn and watching a classmate take a turn.

Resources

A computer game that involves a dance mat and corresponding on-screen dance game

Interactive whiteboard (IWB)

MAIN

- Set up the game so that the dance mat is in front of the IWB and ensure the game is on the easiest level when first introducing to the child.

- Ask the child to choose a friend to come and join in with them using photos on the IWB as suggested in the 'Greetings!' activity.

- Adult models standing on the dance mat and following the on-screen instructions. Draw child's attention to the fact that when a movement is made on the mat it is reflected on the screen. Adult models getting the steps wrong to emphasise this point.

- Ask the child to come and take a turn. Give specific praise for looking at the screen for instructions e.g. 'Great looking at the screen!'

- The children take it in turns to use the dance mat to follow the on-screen instructions. Support them to encourage each other while they are playing.

PLENARY

When it is time to finish the lesson, adult counts down '5, 4, 3, 2, 1, dancing has finished'. Adult models using the mouse to close the program. In subsequent lessons support the child to use the mouse to close the program independently.

CONSOLIDATION ACTIVITIES

On the playground draw out a dance mat similar to the one from the game, using chalk. Support the child to give/follow instructions from a classmate just like in the on-screen game. This will help consolidate the idea that giving instructions from one place can control the actions of a person or object in another place.

79. Cause and Effect

Learning Objective

Emerging

Pupils make connections between control devices and information on screen.

Additional Skills

Attention: accessing an activity for period of time to develop understanding of cause and effect.

Fine motor: using a spacebar, mouse or switch.

Social communication: taking a turn as a pair.

Resources

An online switch, mouse or keyboard-accessible cause and effect game

Access to a computer

A switch (if possible)

MAIN

- If using a switch, set this up so that it works with the chosen game. Ensure that the game is set up and ready to play before asking the child to come and join the lesson.

- Ask the child to choose a friend using the suggestion from 'Greetings!'

- At the computer adult models how to use the game: i.e. press the switch, spacebar or mouse button to operate the online cause and effect game.

- Support the child to use the control device to operate the game and watch the effect of the device on screen.

- Give specific praise e.g. 'Fantastic using the switch!'

- The children take it in turns to use the control device to operate the game.

PLENARY

Adult counts down '5, 4, 3, 2, 1, (game name) has finished', then models using the mouse to close the program. Next time ask the child to use the mouse to close the program.

CONSOLIDATION ACTIVITIES

Whenever it is possible and practical, support the child to use a control device such as the spacebar, mouse or a switch to create an effect on the computer screen e.g. when opening or closing a familiar computer program at the start or end of the lesson.

80. Remote Races

Learning Objective

Emerging

Pupils make connections between control devices and information.

Additional Skills

Fine motor: using the control device.

Visual: watching effects of actions of control device on object.

Social communication: working with a partner.

Resources

Two simple remote control cars (in full working order)

Chalk

Tablet/camera

Switch with 'print' symbol on top and pre-recorded with the word 'switch'

MAIN

- Support the child to choose a friend to come and work with them: this could be done using the suggestion in the 'Greetings!' lesson.

- Adult shows the children the remote control cars and how to use the control device to move them.

- Adult asks the children to draw a race track for the cars using the chalk on the playground floor (or using marker pens and big pieces of paper if in the classroom).

- Once the children have designed the race track, set up the two cars and the start, and support the children to use the control device to move the cars around the track.

- Take photos of the race and of the finish each time the children race the cars around the track.

PLENARY

Look at the photos from the race together on the camera or tablet and support the children to comment on the photos. Ask the child to select a photo they would like printed using the switch. Go and collect the photo from the printer together.

CONSOLIDATION ACTIVITIES

Support the child to use control devices to manipulate other objects or items on screen across the day: e.g. using a remote control to turn a music player or TV on or off; using the mouse to open or close a computer program; using an index finger to swipe or make a choice on a tablet.

81. Control Me

Learning Objective

Developing

Pupils operate some devices independently.

Additional Skills

Visual: matching image to real object.

Attention: waiting for a turn.

Fine motor skills: controlling remote control device.

Resources

Remote control toy (car is ideal)

Exciting toys (disco ball, wind-up toys, beebots, etc.)

Images of each of the toys

Bag

MAIN

- Place the exciting toys around the room. Put all the pictures of the exciting toys into a bag or basket.

- If this is the first time the children have seen the remote control toy, then model to them how it works.

- Explain that the child will pull a picture out the bag, and then they have to direct the remote control toy to find the exciting toy in the room. When they have found it, they can then have a turn at playing with it.

- Each child in the class takes a turn one by one, and once everyone has had a turn, this can be repeated.

- Use the language 'forwards', 'backwards', 'left', 'right', 'under', 'next to', etc. to support mathematical vocabulary development.

PLENARY

Once everyone has had one or two turns, count the children down and ask them to return all of their toys.

CONSOLIDATION ACTIVITIES

Have some remote control toys on offer in the toy basket or free-choice activity so that the children can develop their control of the toys.

82. Registration

Learning Objective

Developing

Pupils use a keyboard to select letters for their own names.

Additional Skills

Visual: finding own name.

Attention: waiting for a turn.

Fine motor skills: pressing keys on keyboard.

Resources

Computer and interactive whiteboard

Laminated name cards

Bag

MAIN

- Place all of the children's name cards into a bag. Have this at the front of the class with everyone sitting in a semicircle around the interactive whiteboard.

- Sing your 'Hello' or 'Good Morning' song and then ask the children 'Who is at school today?'

- Take the bag to one of the children: ask them to find their name card. They take this to the computer. An adult ensures the cursor is in the 'in school today' column. The child types the letters of their name.

- While this is happening, the rest of the class sing the 'Hello' or 'Good Morning' song again and another child takes a turn to look for their name.

- If anyone is not in school that day, the adult writes their name in the 'not at school today' column.

- Once everyone's names are typed, the adult goes through the list to check this. Everyone together counts how many children are at school and not at school. This number is placed at the bottom of the list.

- The adult models to the children saving the document and pressing print.

- One child is selected to go to the printer to get the register.

- This is then placed somewhere in class.

PLENARY

Adult counts the child down '5, 4, 3, 2, 1, registration has finished'.

CONSOLIDATION ACTIVITIES

As the children increase in typing confidence, they can start writing the names of absent friends and the number of children at school today.

83. Names and Games

Learning Objective

Developing

Pupils respond to simple instructions to control a device.

Additional Skills

Visual: recognising pictures and names.

Attention: joining in a group activity for more than 10 minutes.

Social communication: waiting for a turn.

Fine motor: operating a tablet.

Resources

Tablet with a child-friendly playlist of music

Two canvas bags

Pictures with the name of all children in the group

Game names (musical bumps, musical statues, musical chairs, hot potato, etc.)

MAIN

- Place the 'names' bag and the 'games' bag in the centre of the group.

- Ask a child to come and choose a name and game.

- Support the child to read this to the group. It could say 'Alex musical bumps' for example.

- Alex then takes the lead in playing the game. He chooses the song from the playlist and starts and stops the music. Put on a three-minute timer so the child knows how long their turn is.

- Adults are all playing the game too, acting like children. Only offer the child leading the game support if they need this.

- The child then gets a turn at pulling another name and game from the bags and the next person takes a turn.

PLENARY

To calm everyone down after lots of games and dancing, play sleeping lions to support the children to be ready for their next lesson.

CONSOLIDATION ACTIVITIES

Place 'Names and Games' on the children's free-choice activity list so that they can request to play this with their friends at other points once it has been taught.

84. Computer Says Go

Learning Objective

Developing

Pupils use information and communication technology (ICT) to interact with other pupils and adults.

Additional Skills

Visual: recognising actions.

Attention: joining in a group activity for more than 10 minutes.

Social communication: copying adults and peers.

Fine motor skills: operating a screen.

Resources

Computer and interactive whiteboard

Presentation with actions (jump, hop, skip, etc.) and voice naming the actions

MAIN

- This is loosely based on the rules of the game 'Simon Says' but is adapted to use technology.

- The adult models taking the first turn: they stand next to the computer: say, 'Computer says…', and then touch the icon that they want everyone to do (jump, hop, sit down, etc.).

- Everyone carries out the action until another 'Computer says…' action is initiated.

- Each person has three turns and then swaps over.

PLENARY

To calm everyone down after lots of movement, put on some relaxing music for 2 minutes and everyone stays quiet in the room.

CONSOLIDATION ACTIVITIES

Once the children have got an understanding of the rules, you can introduce the component where there is no 'Computer says…' and just the action to try and trick people into carrying out an action when they should have waited.

85. Say Cheese!

Learning Objective

Developing

Pupils use information and communication technology (ICT) to interact with other pupils and adults.

Additional Skills

Social communication: initiating an interaction with a classmate.

Fine motor: operating the buttons on the device.

Visual: looking at a scene and a screen to take a photo.

Resources

Interactive whiteboard (IWB)

A tablet or camera

Photos of classmates

Access to a computer and printer

MAIN

- Adult models for the child how to use the tablet or camera to take a photo, and supports the child to practise using the device to take a photo until they are able to use it independently.

- Ask the child to choose a friend from photos on the IWB.

- Go and find the chosen friend and support the child to ask them to smile for a photo.

- Repeat this for different friends.

- At a computer, model for the child uploading the photos to a file and then printing the pictures.

- Adult supports the child to collect the photos from the printer.

PLENARY

Adult supports the child to share the photos they took with their friends; maybe make a collage or photo book that can be added to by the class.

CONSOLIDATION ACTIVITIES

Place the child's photo book in the class library and encourage the child to share it with their friends or take it home to share their photos with their family.

86. App Writing

Learning Objective

Developing

Pupils use a keyboard or touch screen to select letters and/or images for their own names.

Additional Skills

Attention: maintaining concentration for 5 to 10 minutes.

Social communication: taking a turn with another person.

Fine motor: mark-making with index finger.

Resources

Tablet

An app that allows mark-making on the tablet

MAIN

- Choose an app that allows the child to use an index finger to make marks on the tablet.
- Adult shows the child the app and models writing the first letter of their name.
- Hand the tablet to the child and encourage them to do the same.
- Adult counts down '5, 4, 3, 2, 1, (child's name)'s turn has finished, my turn.' Adult takes back the tablet and models mark-making a pre-writing shape e.g. circle, line.
- Adult counts down '5, 4, 3, 2, 1, my turn finished, your turn.' Gives the tablet back to the child.
- Repeat this turn-taking and mark-making activity.

PLENARY

When it is time to finish, count down '5, 4, 3, 2, 1, tablet writing has finished' and show the child how to close the app. When they are more familiar with this process allow them to close the app independently.

CONSOLIDATION ACTIVITIES

When available, find a similar program compatible with the IWB and support the child to imitate mark-making on the bigger screen.

87. Snack Chat

Learning Objective

Developing

Pupils respond to instructions to control a device.

Additional Skills

Communication: making a request for a required item.

Fine motor: operating the device.

Social communication: making a request.

Resources

Two fully operational walkie-talkies

Snack items

Switch

MAIN

- Introduce the child to the walkie-talkies. Adult models how to use the walkie-talkie, i.e. pressing the button to talk into it, and explore how the sound comes through on the other walkie-talkie.

- Support the child to explore the walkie-talkie and give simple instructions on how to operate e.g. press button, talk.

- Use the walkie-talkies at snack time. Support the child to sit away from the adult with the snacks. Support the child to operate the device and use either speech or a switch to make their snack request. Adult then brings the snack to the child once they have received the request via walkie-talkie.

PLENARY

Adult uses the walkie-talkie to inform the child that snack time has finished e.g. '5, 4, 3, 2, 1, snack time has finished, time for outside.' Support the child to turn off the walkie-talkie, place it somewhere safe and then move onto the next activity.

CONSOLIDATION ACTIVITIES

Support the child to respond to instructions to explore the walkie-talkie in other contexts e.g. when playing outside in the playground.

88. Robots

Learning Objective

Developing

Pupils operate some devices independently.

Additional Skills

Social communication: working as part of a pair.

Gross motor: moving in different directions.

Communication: giving and responding to instructions.

Resources

Laminated 'forwards', 'backwards', 'left' and 'right' symbols (or switches with pre-recorded words and symbols on top)

Chalk

MAIN

- Adult supports the child to choose a friend to take part in the lesson with them.

- On the playground floor use the chalk to draw out a simple road or maze with a start and finish line.

- Adult asks Child B to stand on the start line and supports Child A to use the symbols/speech/switches to instruct Child B to move around the road/maze to the finish line.

- Swap over roles so both children have a turn controlling their robot friend.

- Encourage the children to move like robots!

PLENARY

Support Child A to direct Child B back to the classroom using the symbols/speech/switches and then Child B to direct Child A back to their seat.

CONSOLIDATION ACTIVITIES

If possible use a remote control car in a similar way with Child A directing Child B on how to move the car and then swap roles.

89. Questions on Camera

Learning Objective

Developing

Pupils use ICT to communicate meaning and express ideas in a variety of contexts.

Additional Skills

Visual: developing filming skills.

Attention: working with a partner.

Social communication: asking questions.

Resources

Tablet device for each child with parental controls turned on

List of questions

MAIN

- Working in pairs, one person is the recorder and the other the actor.

- The recorder uses a tablet device to film asking the actor some 'what/where' questions such as 'What is your name?', 'What is your favourite colour?' and 'What did you do at the weekend?'

- If verbal language is not used, the recorder can use whatever communication strategy they have to ask the questions: this may need to be supported by the adults.

- Once the questions have been asked, together the pair watch the video.

- They then swap over and take on the other roles.

PLENARY

Once everyone in the class has finished their videos, these are all uploaded to the class computer. Everyone sits and watches the videos together.

CONSOLIDATION ACTIVITIES

Whenever the children get a chance to film something, ensure that they can. This will help them practise keeping the image in the centre of the shot, holding the recording device still and being an appropriate distance from the action.

90. Put It in the Diary

Learning Objective

Developing

Pupils begin to choose equipment and software for a familiar activity.

Additional Skills

Visual: typing on a keyboard.

Attention: persisting at a task until the end.

Social communication: conveying information clearly.

Resources

Access to tablet devices and computers with word processing

Paper and pens to create an 'in activity checklist'

MAIN

- At a time of celebration, this could be a religious event, public holiday or class birthday: ask each of the children to use ICT to let someone else in the school know the details of the party.

- Explain that the children can choose to make a video with the details, take photos or write using a publishing program.

- Before everyone starts creating, work as a group to establish the key facts such as the location, time and date. Write these out for each of the children on an 'in activity checklist' so that they can self-check the details.

- Give each child access to the technology they need for their preferred method of communication.

- Adults to support where needed.

- When the child has finished, refer them back to the 'in activity checklist' to ensure that all the key details are included.

PLENARY

Once everyone in the group has completed their invitation, they need to be delivered. This will also give a chance for children to see that you can print some things and hand-deliver, while others need to be sent electronically.

CONSOLIDATION ACTIVITIES

Keep a record of the different ways that the children choose to create communication material. Encourage them to try different methods at various times. This can also be used to create messages about what is happening in the class that could be put on the school website.

91. This Is My Favourite

Learning Objective

Developing

Pupils gather information from different sources.

Additional Skills

Visual: search and locating desired content.

Attention: sharing attention in a group.

Social communication: taking interest in others' likes.

Resources

Tablet device for each child with parental controls turned on

List of questions

MAIN

- Each child in the group is given a tablet computer.

- The lead adult shows the children a list of questions. These might include 'What is your favourite cartoon video clip?', 'What is your favourite song?' and 'What city/town/village do you live in?'

- One question at a time, the children need to open an appropriate app or website to be able to demonstrate the answers to the questions.

- Children are given time to search for each of these one by one. They are then asked to show everyone in their group what they have found for 1 minute.

- The next question is then asked.

PLENARY

Once everyone has answered the questions and shared their content with the others in the group, ask the children to close the applications and lock their tablet and place it back on charge.

CONSOLIDATION ACTIVITIES

Create a display with the children of the different programs, websites and applications that we all use for searching for different items. This will then include environmental print labels for familiar brands, and screen shots of the children's favourite content.

92. My Learning Journey

Learning Objective

Developing

Pupils use ICT to communicate meaning and express their ideas in a variety of contexts.

Additional Skills

Communication: making a choice between two or more photos.

Social communication: commenting on past events.

Fine motor: scissor and sticking skills.

Resources

Access to a computer with keyboard and mouse (or a tablet)

A computer file with photos from child's week e.g. of them painting and playing

Access to a printer

Scissors appropriate for child's grip

Glue

Scrapbook/large notebook

MAIN

- At the end of the week ask the child to come to the computer e.g. on a Friday morning or afternoon. Adult explains that we are going to make a book about our learning and it is the child's job to choose the photos to go in this book.

- Adult models for the child using the mouse to scroll through photos, click on them and then decide to print or not. Adult models how to print the photo (this can be supported with symbol instructions).

- Adult supports the child to select four or five photos from their week. When looking at the photos adult supports the child to comment on them: e.g. 'I see sand', 'I like building' and 'I play with Louis.'

- Adult and child go to the printer to collect the chosen photos.

- Back in the classroom cut the photos out and stick them in the scrapbook to begin a learning journey book developed by the child.

PLENARY

When the photos have been stuck into the learning journey go back to the computer. Adult models finding the first letter of the child's name and typing it. Support the child to find as many letters from their name as possible and print this out to stick in the book alongside the photos.

CONSOLIDATION ACTIVITIES

Send the book home with the child to look at over the weekend with their family. Ask the family to also take pictures and add to the book at home together, with the child choosing the photos from a computer, tablet or smartphone.

92. My Learning Journey *cont.*

Teaching note: if the process of printing the photo is not yet a possibility for the child, set up a switch with a 'print' symbol on top and pre-recorded with the word 'print'. Support the child to use the switch to request when they want a photo printed.

93. Ultimate Toy

Learning Objective

Developing

Pupils gather information from different sources.

Additional Skills

Fine motor: cutting and sticking skills.

Communication: communicating ideas to others.

Social communication: listening/commenting on the ideas of others.

Resources

Access to an Internet search engine and printer

Toy and large shop catalogues

Photos of toys from around the school/ classroom

Actual toys

A4 paper – this could be a template for designing a toy or act as a design board

Glue

Scissors

MAIN

- Adult explains that we are going to design our own toy! We will need to look at different pictures from different places to get ideas.

- Lesson/activity 1: adult models using a computer or tablet to search for, say, their best toy, selecting a photo for a reason, such as the colour and printing the photo. Support the child to do the same, finding photos of preferred toys for different reasons and sticking them onto their design board.

- Lesson/activity 2: adult models looking through the catalogues, finding pictures of toys they like, explaining reason, cutting out the pictures and sticking them onto their design board.

- Lesson/activity 3: adult models looking at pictures of toys from around the classroom, selecting one or two, explains why they like them and then cuts out the picture to add to design board.

- Lesson/activity 4: look at actual toys from classroom: draw on design board the favourite part of toy.

- Once child has gathered all the information about what they like best about toys from different sources; support them to draw and design their ultimate toy.

PLENARY

At the end of each lesson support the children to come together as a group and look at each other's design boards. Encourage the children to comment on the different ideas on the boards about what they like/ don't like.

When the children have completed their own design of the ultimate toy, share these with the group in a similar way.

93. Ultimate Toy *cont.*

CONSOLIDATION ACTIVITIES

Follow a similar process for other lessons and activities across the curriculum e.g. the ultimate cake/sandwich/ class trip/ pet house.

Teaching note: this activity might work best as a series of lessons or as a carousel where the children move around the different sources of information.

94. Occasion Celebration

Learning Objective

Developing

Pupils begin to choose software and equipment for a familiar activity.

Additional Skills

Fine motor: operating chosen equipment or software.

Social communication: expressing an opinion or making a comment.

Communication: making a choice between two or more items of equipment or software.

Resources

Access to symbol-writing program

Switches

Pens and paper

Tablet/video-recording device

Choosing board

Laminated symbols of above software and equipment

MAIN

- Ask the children to come and sit in a semicircle.

- Adult explains that we are going to make Christmas (or another holiday) greetings for our families.

- Adult explains we need to decide how we are going to make our Christmas greetings. Adult models using the different software and equipment available e.g. using the symbol-writing program to write a message and using the tablet to record a video message.

- Adult offers the choosing board (with the laminated symbols of the available software and equipment) to the children and encourages them to make a choice.

- Adults support the children to use their chosen software or equipment to make a Christmas greeting for someone at home (or it can be for a friend in another class).

PLENARY

Once the greetings messages are complete support the children to share them with their families at home or with their friend in another class – this might mean playing back a video greeting, reading the symbol greetings or pressing the switch to hear the greeting.

CONSOLIDATION ACTIVITIES

Use a similar approach for other occasions across the year e.g. birthday, Valentine's Day, Easter.

95. Take That

Learning Objective

Developing

Pupils use ICT to communicate and present their ideas.

Additional Skills

Visual: searching for and locating desired content.

Attention: working for an extended period to complete a task.

Fine motor: using scissors.

Auditory: listening to two- to three-part instructions.

Resources

Tablet device for each child with parental controls turned on

Selection of famous self-portraits on the interactive whiteboard

Access to printer

Paper

Scissors

Glue

MAIN

- This ICT session is going to be combined with an art session.

- Show the children lots of self-portraits of famous artists on the interactive whiteboard. Ensure that you show a range that includes traditional and contemporary pieces.

- Tell the children that the only equipment they have is a tablet, printer, glue and paper in order to make their own self-portrait.

- Lead adult to model an option if they think the children will need higher levels of support. This can include finding images using a search engine or taking photos using the tablet.

- These are all sent to the printer (or the tablet is attached to a computer and then it is sent to the printer).

- Once each child has a selection of images and photos, they can then put the tablets away and begin using the art materials to compose their portrait.

- Encourage the children to cut and place the items and move them around before sticking them on the paper.

- Once everyone is happy with his or her portrait, tidy away the materials and lay them out for everyone to see.

PLENARY

Children to take a photo of their portrait using the tablet. Support the children to comment on their self-portraits.

95. Take That *cont.*

CONSOLIDATION ACTIVITIES

Using the photos taken of the portraits, photos that adults may have taken of the children as they went through the process, and any real artwork, spend time with the children making a classroom display of their ICT artwork.

96. Character Match

Learning Objective

Securing

Pupils find similar information in different formats.

Additional Skills

Visual: searching for appropriate content.

Social communication: sharing information about an interest.

Fine motor skills: operating a tablet.

Resources

Tablet with parental controls turned on

Selection of magazines with familiar/popular cartoon characters

MAIN

- Place a range of cartoon magazines in the centre of the group.

- Allow the children to spend time exploring the magazines. Ask questions about the characters and what is happening in the pictures.

- Ask every child to choose their favourite character and find a page with the character on it.

- Tell everyone that they are now going to use the Internet to find the same character by using a search engine.

- Each child to have a tablet device, and the adult to offer verbal instruction and model the process of turning the correct application on and going to the web browser if appropriate.

- Allow the children some time to see how much they can do for themselves.

- The children may need some help with the characters' names; adults to point to the spelling of it in the magazine or write this on a whiteboard so that they can copy this.

- When everyone has found a picture, these can be shared as a group, and the child can tell everyone why they chose that character.

PLENARY

Count down '5, 4, 3, 2, 1' and ask the children to turn off the tablets and place them back in the charging deck.

CONSOLIDATION ACTIVITIES

Encourage the children to look at other forms of media as much as possible so that they can make connections. This can be by seeing an article in the newspaper and looking this up online, or researching a trip and matching this to the information leaflet.

97. Find That Tune

Learning Objective

Securing

Pupils can load a resource and make a choice from it.

Additional Skills

Visual: following picture instructions.

Attention: joining in a group activity for more than 10 minutes.

Social communication: waiting for a turn.

Fine motor skills: operating a tablet.

Resources

Tablet with a child-friendly playlist of music

Picture instructions showing the steps to locate a preferred song

MAIN

- Have the tablet device pre-loaded with a playlist of the children's favourite songs.

- Model to the group following the picture instructions to load and choose a song.

- Adult to select a child to come and take a turn at playing the music: this can be in preparation for a future party or event.

- Allow the child time to follow the visuals and select the appropriate program and then the song.

- Once the song is playing, everyone join in dancing games.

- Provide the child with a two-minute timer so that they know when their turn is up.

- They can choose the next person to take a turn.

- Before the turn, adult to ensure tablet and program have been turned off and ready for the next person to follow the instructions.

PLENARY

After everyone has had a turn, play a relaxing piece of music to help everyone to calm down before the next lesson.

CONSOLIDATION ACTIVITIES

At a group party or event, the children can be in charge of the music. Use timers of 10 minutes so that they know when their turn has ended.

98. Transition Times

Learning Objective

Securing

Pupils use ICT to communicate and present their ideas.

Additional Skills

Communication: indicating preferences.

Kinaesthetic: moving around new environments.

Fine motor: operating a device to take photos.

Resources

Camera

Access to printer

Laminated 'like', 'don't like', 'don't know' symbols

Five laminated symbols of activities/items the child definitely does and doesn't like

Three A4 black pieces of paper

MAIN

- Towards the middle of the summer term explain to the child they are going to visit their new class or school.

- Explain they will have a camera to take photos of their new class/school: then we will talk about parts of the school the child liked or didn't like.

- Visit the child's new class/school and support them to take photos of their new environment.

- Support the child to take the photos off the camera and print them out.

- At a table back in a familiar environment lay out the three pieces of black A4 paper and place the 'like', 'don't like' and 'don't know' symbols on each piece of paper.

- Adult models for the child looking at one of the five laminated symbols and deciding if they like/don't like or don't know how they feel about the item on the symbol and then placing it on the respective A4 piece of paper; e.g. if the symbol was baked beans the adult might say 'I don't like baked beans' and place the symbol on the piece of paper with the 'don't like' symbol.

- Support the child to sort the rest of the laminated symbols in the same way (this is to ensure the child understands the process of expressing how they feel about items/activities).

- Adult then shows the child the photos they took on their visit to their new class/school and supports the child to sort them onto the three A4 pieces of paper, expressing whether they liked, didn't like or didn't know how they felt about items in the photos.

98. Transition Times *cont.*

PLENARY

Adult supports the child to look at the photos they have sorted and talk about how they have expressed their ideas; e.g. if the child has put photos of the new teacher on the 'like' piece of paper ask the child to comment on this, and if they put photos of the chairs in the new classroom on the 'don't like' piece of paper talk about why they don't like them.

CONSOLIDATION ACTIVITIES

This process could be used to support the child to express their ideas about a variety of activities or environments across the day e.g. the lunch hall, the playground and different curriculum subjects.

Teaching note: supporting the child to use a camera to take photos and then express their ideas can support teachers to develop meaningful transition programmes for children. If used in other contexts it can support teachers to adapt the environment to better support the child's learning.

99. Hey Mr DJ!

Learning Objective

Securing

Pupils can load a resource and make a choice from it.

Additional Skills

Communication: responding to requests from peers.

Fine motor: operating a device such as a mouse or tablet.

Social communication: taking part in a group activity.

Kinaesthetic: moving and dancing with classmates.

Resources

Tablet or computer with access to a pre-made appropriate playlist

MAIN

- Explain to the child that they are going to be responsible for selecting and playing the music for a party (or a PE session, free time, etc.).

- With the child, set up the tablet or computer with a pre-made playlist and support the child to operate the device to choose a song.

- During the activity encourage the child to make selections to keep their classmates moving and dancing.

- Encourage the other children to make requests of the 'DJ' and support the child to find the songs their classmates have asked for.

PLENARY

Support the child to be in charge of a game such as 'Musical Chairs' operating the device to stop and start so that the game can be played.

CONSOLIDATION ACTIVITIES

Across the day ask the child to set up different sessions on the computer so that they practise loading a resource and then making a choice e.g. opening PowerPoint and finding the 'Greetings!' slideshow for the beginning of the day.

100. Read All About It!

Learning Objective

Securing

Pupils find similar information in different formats.

Additional Skills

Social communication: working as part of a pair.

Communication: expressing ideas to others.

Kinaesthetic: moving around the classroom and school to find information.

Fine motor: collating different information through cutting and sticking.

Resources

Examples of child-appropriate newspaper stories

Newspaper page templates

Glue

Scissors

MAIN

- Explain to the children we are going to make a class newspaper about our topic (this works well with topics such as the Romans, World War II and the Great Fire of London). Adult shows some examples of newspaper stories and explains how the information comes from different sources i.e. the Internet, photographs, interviews, TV, books, etc.

- Adult explains that each child is going to make a story about our topic and they have to find information from different sources. Ask children for ideas about where they could find information e.g. the Internet, school library, TV.

- Ask the children to work in pairs and adults support the children to find different sources to make their story e.g. go to the library and find a book about the topic and photocopy an interesting page.

- Eventually put all the information together, say by sticking the photocopies, printed information, etc. onto paper to make the news story.

- Put all the pages together to make a class newspaper about the topic.

PLENARY

At the end of each session ask each pair to come to the front of the class and share the information they have found and where they found it. When the newspaper is complete look at it all together and comment on the different information.

CONSOLIDATION ACTIVITIES

Whenever starting a new topic, encourage the children to do their own research first by using the Internet, the library, finding TV programmes, etc. and encourage them to feed back their findings to their classmates.

101. Walkie-Talkie Wondering

Learning Objective

Securing

Pupils use ICT to communicate and present their ideas.

Additional Skills

Fine motor: operating a walkie-talkie.

Communication: using preferred method of communication to express an idea.

Social communication: listening and responding to a partner.

Kinaesthetic: moving around the school building.

Resources

Puzzle pieces that make up a complete puzzle (how many depends on how long you wish the activity to last!)

Two walkie-talkies in full working order

Laminated symbols/ photos of different areas of the school

Switch (if needed by the child to communicate)

Camera/tablet

MAIN

- Support the child to choose a partner for this lesson.

- Adult shows the children the puzzle pieces and explains that Child A will hide a puzzle piece somewhere in the school and will use the walkie-talkie to tell Child B where that is. Child B will then run and find the puzzle piece while Child A goes on to hide the next piece. This will continue until all the puzzle pieces have been hidden and then found again.

- Adults support Child A and Child B to take part in the lesson. If needed the adult can support Child A to choose their next hiding location by showing them the laminated symbols/photos of different areas of the school and supporting them to make a choice.

- Once all the puzzle pieces have been found, Child A and Child B swap roles and take part in the lesson again.

PLENARY

When the children return to the classroom, support them to complete the puzzle together and then use a camera or tablet to take a photo of the completed puzzle this could then be added to their learning journey that week.

CONSOLIDATION ACTIVITIES

The walkie-talkies could also be used during playtime as part of a game of hide and seek.

Teaching note: if the child has difficulties speaking into the walkie-talkie the adult can use the switch to pre-record the name of the location that the child can then press to communicate with their friend via the walkie-talkie.